Edward Edwards

Chapters of the Biographical History of the French Academy

With an Appendix Relating to the Unpublished Monastic Chronicle....

Edward Edwards

Chapters of the Biographical History of the French Academy
With an Appendix Relating to the Unpublished Monastic Chronicle....

ISBN/EAN: 9783337014605

Printed in Europe, USA, Canada, Australia, Japan

Cover: Foto ©ninafisch / pixelio.de

More available books at **www.hansebooks.com**

CHAPTERS

OF THE

BIOGRAPHICAL HISTORY

OF THE

FRENCH ACADEMY.

WITH AN APPENDIX.
RELATING TO THE UNPUBLISHED MONASTIC CHRONICLE.
ENTITLED,

LIBER DE HYDA.

By

EDWARD EDWARDS.

NEW YORK:
G. P. PHILES AND CO., 64, NASSAU STREET.
1864.

CONTENTS.

----- -- — —

II. THE EARLY BIOGRAPHERS OF KING ALFRED; WITH
    SOME ACCOUNT OF AN UNPRINTED CHRONICLE
    OF ANGLO-SAXON HISTORY.

"True, indeed, it is
That they whom Death has hidden from our sight
Are worthiest of the mind's regard; with these
The Future cannot contradict the Past:
Mortality's last exercise and proof
Is undergone; the transit made that shows
The very Soul, revealed as she departs.
Yet (as you have suggested),—I shall give,—
Whilst we descend into those silent vaults,—
Some pictures from the Living."

The Excursion, v.

CHAPTER I.

RETROSPECTIVE GLANCES AT THE GENERAL HISTORY OF *THE FRENCH ACADEMY*, AND AT ITS INFLUENCE ON FRENCH LITERATURE.

On this side the Channel, we have been accustomed to think of endowed and privileged literary associations, as of a somewhat cumbrous machinery for thrusting the heads of dwarfs up to a temporary level with the heads of great men. We cannot, or cannot very easily, enter into the views and feelings with which many highly educated and accomplished Frenchmen will talk of the private doings, and of the public displays of the "French Academy." When we find a man of the world, and a statesman—as well as a distinguished author—like the Count de Montalembert, writing (as he wrote in 1863) of the membership of the French Academy, as being "the noblest reward which, in our days, can crown a glorious and independent life," we are apt to regard it as, at all events, a highly rhetorical phrase. The flutter of excitement which an academical election in Paris often creates, amongst the men of high scholarship, and of varied experience of life, as well as amongst the fashionable writers of the passing day, seems to us overstrained, if it be not puerile. And we cannot forget that in some well-known instances, elsewhere than in France, academic honours have served to drape very poor performances in showy costumes.

The beset-
ting sins of
literary aca-
demies.
When the institution from whose history it is the object of these pages to select some salient chapters, was yet in its cradle, the witty epistolographer Balzac wrote to his friend Chapelain :—" You tell me you have been received into the '*Academie des beaux esprits.*' May I ask who are those '*beaux esprits*' who have received you ?" Balzac's inquiry points, with quiet sarcasm, to a reproach to which learned academicians, in all countries, have frequently laid themselves open. An association exclusively composed of men of great genius, and of lofty ambition, would be, indeed,

" A monster, which the world ne'er saw."

An association of mixed materials, including, as it needs must include, men of small parts, and of petty aims in life, is sure to possess a tendency towards the fostering of mediocrity, the growth of servility, and the pedantic display of minute learning. But, whether such tendencies shall, in the long run, be developed, or be held in check, seems to me to be a question, partly, perhaps, of organization, but partly of social atmosphere.

If, from the days of the *Intronati* of Sienna, and the *Infiammati* of Padua, downwards, literary history abounds with instances in which the lower elements of learned Corporations—as of Corporations unlearned—have become dominant over the higher, it also tells us of Academies which have done their proper conjunctive work with eminent success, and have, at the same time, so governed themselves as to make the nobler qualities and aspirations of their members bear rule over the less noble. Organize a learned Academy as you will, small corporate interests and small personal temptations will, occasionally, give birth to cabals

and cliques. In cliques, you will be sure to find worship-
pers of success, however obtained, and tools of power,
however directed. But in some "Academies" these baser
spirits are found to run riot; in others they are habitually
kept under. Hence it is that I think the present topic
one which may be usefully treated. It is also a topic which
may reasonably be thought to need no extraordinary ability,
or exceptional advantages, in order to its useful treatment.
One special advantage, indeed, it possesses—in itself—for
the present writer. It is, so far as is known to me, un-
touched in English literature. And the freshness of a
subject tends powerfully to eke out humble means of
handling it.

There will, I think, be little difficulty in showing that
even in times which try, most searchingly, of what sort of
clay men are made, the French Academy has inhaled, freely,
the wholesome air of public opinion; and has used its pri-
vileges, its endowments, and its reputation, on behalf of the
great permanent interests of Society at large. It has
—if I have at all read its history aright—set a good example to institutions more important, but not less assailable,
than itself. If this can truthfully be said of a privileged
society, which had Richelieu for its founder, Lewis XIV
for its benefactor, and Napoleon I for its re-organizer, it
may fairly seem probable that our current insular opinion
concerning literary Academies lies open to some degree of
revision. And, perhaps, it may appear, in the sequel of this
narrative, that passing circumstances add something of
immediate interest and piquancy to this topic, for English
readers, as well as for their neighbours.

The Academy's history begins with the obscure meetings
of a small knot of men, whose chief link of sympathy was

a love of literature, and a love of mutual praise. Meetings, truly, of a sort to which scores of parallels might be found, in almost all countries, and at almost all periods. It is no sooner incorporated than it is plunged into literary controversy. The first public appearance of the new Academy exhibits it as the critical assailant of one of the most famous works in French literature. For some time it threatens to follow in the too easy steps of the many societies which have bartered servility for privilege, and praise for pelf. But, after much conflict, the Academic arena becomes an instrument for ventilating and for disseminating thoughts which were destined to germinate far and wide, and to be fruitful in ultimate good, even when seeming to aggravate present evil. Most of all, it becomes, at length, one of the main appliances, by means of which the greatest achievements of intellects that were strong enough to press through all obstacles, are made to arouse, to stimulate and to cheer, other intellects, not quite so robust—it may be—and still struggling in the crowd, but rich in promise and in latent power. And this I call the special corporate work of every literary Academy worthy of its name.

Sources of the Academy's history.

It may deserve remark that, even for French readers, the story of the French Academy, as a whole, has yet to be told. Pellisson has narrated its origin and beginnings with loving minuteness, and with a grace of style of which even foreigners can feel the charm. But he stops, almost at the threshold, with the year 1652. D'Olivet continued the narrative, but with much less attractiveness, up to 1700. D'Alembert, as is well known, wrote a long and able series of memoirs of individual Academicians, in which much of the history of the institution is embodied. Other materials abound, but they are widely scattered. The voluminous collections of the Academy itself, the literary journals of two centuries, the lives, diaries, and correspondence of men of letters and publicists, contain materials which might be made to yield vivid illustrations of the progress and influence of a society whose history, in an unusual degree, mirrors the intellectual life of France, at the critical periods of French culture. Nor would such a narrative be simply a contribution to the mental history of France. The impulsive and the modifying powers of a body like the French Academy are manifold, and, in their results, stretch far beyond the limits of its immediate sphere. The influences of such an institution upon language; upon the fortunes of books; upon the tendencies of nascent literary ambition; upon the rewards of that ambition, when it has found its appropriate field of labour; upon the relations between the men of thought and the men of action;—these are all questions of a more than merely national interest, and upon all of them such a narrative, if well written, may throw valuable light. It is a contribution to what our German friends call the " History of Culture," which I would gladly see made.

Here, of course, I can attempt no such task, even in outline. I must content myself with a few individual figures and a few groups, chosen from among the more conspicuous personages and incidents of the untold story.

CHAPTER II.

THE FOUNDERS — THE HOTEL DE RAMBOUILLET — THE ACADEMY INCORPORATED — THE QUARREL CONCERNING *THE CID.*

ABOUT the year 1629, a few Parisian acquaintances began to gather periodically around the table of Valentine Conrart, one of the king's secretaries, but chiefly remarkable for his liberal mind, and his passionate love of literature.   Conrart wished to establish frequent social meetings, at which books and ideas might be talked of, rather than events and reputations.   Literary Academies had long been prevalent in Italy, and some of them had acquired great renown.   By this time, the desire for something of the same sort in France seems to have been floating in the air, and might have germinated almost anywhere, as chance directed. Ménage had not yet established his " Wednesdays," so frequently mentioned in the correspondence of the middle of the century, nor Mlle. de Scudéri those " Saturdays " which occupy so prominent a place in the chronicles of the *précieux* and the *précieuses*.   But Colletet had his literary gatherings, as well as Conrart.   And Death had only just closed Malherbe's humble apartment, on the outside of which courtly aspirants—patient, although eager for admission—had to wait, because, as he was wont to tell them through the closed door, the chairs were all occupied within. Mlle. de Gournay, too, had her frequent receptions for the worship of Montaigne, for the admiring perusal of her own extensive correspondence, and for the elaborate defence of those beloved archaisms which the rising tide of literary innovation was threatening to sweep away.

The Conversazioni of Valentine Conrart.

Still more attractive were the assemblies of the Hotel de Rambouillet, the centre of all that was refined and fashionable in the Paris of the day, where plays and banquets, surprises and masquerades, took their turn with the more sober enjoyments of readings and conversation, and where the puerilities and the pedantries which so easily gather around a literary coterie were somewhat kept down by the frequent presence of men of long experience in the council and the camp.

The Hotel de Rambouillet.

But, despite that partial restraint, it may with truth be asserted that most of the intimates of the Hotel de Rambouillet left their everyday existence at its doors as they entered, and became, for the time, mere personages of romance. In their hands, literature lost its needful curbs and its wholesome dependence on ordinary sympathies and common interests. It ceased to breathe the bracing air of public opinion, and was coddled into sickliness by the heated and perfumed atmosphere of that splendid circle, which is now chiefly remembered by bibliomaniacs, when they turn over the leaves of the coveted rarity entitled, *La Guirlande de Julie.* Even within its own generation, the day came when almost the sole results of those brilliant, ambitious, and long-continued gatherings were, on the one hand, the interminable *Clelias,* and *Grand Cyruses,* of Mlle. de Scuderi, and her many imitators; and on the other *Les Précieuses Ridicules* of Moliere.

Conrart's quiet gatherings made no pretensions to vie with such gay entertainments as these. But they had their share of small affectations, and many of the members were versifiers of that unhappy order whose productions are remembered only because they have been piquantly embalmed by the satirists of another generation. The most distinguished member of the circle was Jean Chapelain, who

The small poets of Lewis XIV day.

would have died, as he had long lived, with the reputation of being a great but very modest poet, had he not, unluckily, been prevailed upon, at length, to give his poem to the press. He sold six editions within a few months, and not a single copy ever afterwards.

These assemblies would probably have continued their unassuming course, but for the intervention of Richelieu, whose curiosity had been excited by some rumour of their pursuits, and who, after he had made repeated inquiries about the members, signified his desire to become their patron, and to cause their incorporation.

Richelieu
hears of the
infant Aca-
demy,

Those who love to discover mean motives for pregnant deeds have often represented Richelieu's anxiety to create the Academy as arising from a desire to enslave literature, just say they, as he had already enslaved France. More recently, Michelet has stigmatised him as bent on confining the Academicians to mere "word-polishing," to the exclusion of all commerce with ideas. But neither charge is sustained by the evidence. Nor was Richelieu usually so little skilled in shaping his means to his ends. That love of learning which made him take an intense interest in the fortunes of the drama, at a moment when he was at once struggling with court conspiracies, and opening a new campaign against Spain, may well suggest the possibility that he foresaw something of the future of French literature, and may have anticipated the glory of at least connecting his name with its history, even if he should fail in his efforts to make personal contribution to its enduring treasures. The bare name of a "man of letters" was always a sufficient claim to Richelieu's courteous attention. To those who bore it worthily he showed marks of respect which he seems never to have accorded to mere rank. If he listened,

And re-
solves to in-
corporate it.

Richelieu's
sincere love
of letters.

with some impatience, to strictures on his own dramatic
plots, he bore no grudge to his critics. When, for example, he had, on one occasion, angrily torn in pieces an
elaborate criticism on his ' *Grande Pastorale*,' he caused
the fragments to be carefully put together, spent great part
of the night in pondering them, and then sent to thank
the critic for his advice, which, he said, he would follow,
being convinced that "they understood such matters better
than he did." This was not the way of a man who wished
to have about him mere puppets, whose strings he might
pull at pleasure.

The letters-patent were drawn up in January, 1635, and
were sealed by Chancellor Séguier, who expressed his wish
to become a member. When sent to the Parliament to be
registered, they met with violent opposition. To some of
the lawyers it is evident that the occasion was but a pre-
text. They disliked the Academy because they hated its
patron. Others seem really to have feared that the new
institution was to be used as a political weapon. They
imagined that, when once established, its functions might,
possibly, be modified at the will of the patron, until it
should become a dangerous rival to the old tribunals.
Others, again, who were in the daily habit of taking great
liberties with the French language, looked jealously at the
rise of a corporation avowedly created for its protection.
One learned councillor—the father of the satirist Scarron—
resented the proposal as an attack on the Parliament's
dignity. It reminded him, he said, of that Roman Emperor who, after stripping the Senate of all power over
public business, sent to ask its opinion as to the best
method of dressing a turbot. At last, Richelieu himself
had to write a letter to the Parliament explanatory of
the Academy's objects; and so, after a delay of two

The issue
of the letters-
patent.

The preju-
dices of the
lawyers
against the
new
Academy.

years and a half, the registration was effected, but only after the insertion of a cautious proviso " that the members of the said Academy shall concern themselves only with such books as shall be either written by themselves, or submitted to them by the authors thereof."

Prejudice against the new establishment was not confined to the lawyers. Strange rumours as to its purpose were spread about the city. The popular cry against 'Monopoly' which, a year or two later, raised such turbulent crowds in the streets of London, and had such memorable consequences, was applied in Paris to the harmless Academicians. A diarist of the day has recorded that a man who had just contracted to take a house, near that in which their early meetings were held, having inquired the cause of an unusual concourse of carriages which had attracted his attention, refused to carry out his bargain, because, said he, " I will not live in a street in which there is to be every week a ' *Cademie de Manopoleurs*.' "

The letters-patent and the statutes.

Whilst the registration of the letters-patent was yet pending, the statutes had been drawn up, and had received Richelieu's sanction. The only change he made in them was to strike out a silly clause engaging each Academician " *to revere the virtues and memory of their Protector*." Pellisson has preserved a sort of preface intended to accompany the statutes, but not published, which may serve to show what were the anticipations of the original members. " Our language," it is there said, " already more perfect than any other living tongue, may well, in course of time, succeed the Latin, as the Latin succeeded the Greek, provided greater care than heretofore be taken of the elocution. . . . Let it be the function of the Academicians to purify the language from the barbarisms it has contracted, whether in the mouths of the populace or in the throng of the law-courts *(dans la foule du Palais)*, and amidst the impurities of chicanery ; or by the bad customs of ignorant courtiers ; or by the abuses of those who write it corruptly, or who utter in the pulpits what ought, indeed, to be said, but is said in a wrong way."

The number of the Academicians was fixed at forty. In order to an election or an exclusion, twenty must be present ; the votes must be taken by ballot; and the majority must not be less than four. A perpetual secretary, a director, and a chancellor, each serving for two months, and re-eligible, are also to be chosen by ballot. The choice of new members is to have the sanction of the Protector. The only other restrictive condition is that the members shall be " *de bonnes mœurs, de bonne réputation, de bon esprit, et propres aux fonctions académiques.*" The ordinary meetings are to be held once a week. The chief functions of the Academy, it is enacted, shall be " to labour with all possible care and diligence to give fixed rules to the language, and to make it more eloquent, and fitter for the treatment of the arts and sciences." The best authors are to be distributed amongst the Academicians, in order that such rules may be elicited. A Dictionary, a Grammar, a systematic treatise on Rhetoric, and another on Poetry, are to be composed. A discourse on some subject chosen by the Academy is to be made, weekly, by each Academician in turn. All works submitted to the Academy's judgment are to be referred to the examination of a committee, who shall report to the whole body, for its decision. *The special duty imposed on the Academy.*

Almost as soon as Richelieu's proposal had been accepted, sixteen new Academicians were added to the original eleven. Boisrobert, one of the Cardinal's confidants, was zealous in beating for recruits, and, in the opinion of some of his colleagues, was only too successful. Chapelain was more chary of the honour, but was very anxious to enlist Balzac, that prince of phrasemaking epistolographers, who, for a while, coquetted with the proffer. "Whatever you may say," he wrote to his inviter, "I am afraid you will not persuade me. It will be difficult for me to adore that rising sun you speak of. I am told that it is to be a tyranny ruling over minds, to which we book-makers must give blind obedience. If that be so, I am a rebel." Chapelain replies that it is not so, at all; that the alarms are quite groundless, and that his correspondent must be elected immediately. The affair now wears a new aspect. Balzac begins to perceive that "this new society will do honour to France, will make Italy jealous, and—if I have any skill in horoscope—will soon become the oracle of civilized Europe." But he still complains that the Academy includes some members who are only qualified to act as "beadles" to it, and begs that at least there may be two classes of members, so that "the patricians shall be separated from the mob." He is forced, however, to be content with a place among the crowd. Other new members are elected, during 1634 and 1635, which raise the number to thirty-nine. The most distinguished of them were Voiture, De Vaugelas, Cureau de la Chambre, and Pierre Séguier, Chancellor of France. The Academy began the exercise of its public functions amidst a literary storm, the circumstances of which are, perhaps, curious enough to warrant a digression.

The appearance of *The Cid*, a few months before the registration of the Academy's letters-patent, had been welcomed by the public with enthusiasm. But the public had been almost as enthusiastic, a little earlier, about Mairet's *Sophonisbe*, and even about Tristan's *Marianne*. The no-

The correspondence of Chapelain with Balzac.

The controversy about The Cid

proverbial " *C'est beau comme le Cid*," might, perchance, prove as short-lived as the " *C'est du Godeau* " had been. At all events, the many rivals whom Corneille's success threw into the shade, were eager to prove to the public that what pleased it so mightily ought not to have pleased it at all ; that the very subject was totally unfitted for the drama, and the execution opposed to all the "rules of art." Georges de Scudéri was foremost in taking the field.   He had already written a dozen tragi-comedies, abounding in affectation, puerilities, and bad taste of all kinds, but regarded by himself as precious gifts, for which the public was bound to be the more grateful, as coming from one of a family in which, until then, " *on n'avait jamais eu de plume qu'au chapeau*." He began his attack by undertaking to prove that " the plot of *The Cid* is worthless ;" that " the play offends against the chief rules of dramatic poetry, and that it contains a multitude of bad verses ;" and he finally alleges that " almost all such beauties as it has are stolen." Lest any one should think it possible that some spice of envy might be mixed up with so trenchant a criticism, he conjures the reader " to believe that so base a vice is not in my nature.   Being what I am, if I had any ambition, it would aim at something loftier than the renown of this author." Such a programme and such an asseveration exhibit the assailant.   He was silly enough not to stop even there.   He sent Corneille a letter which read like a challenge.   " There is no need," replied the poet, " to ascertain whether you or I be the most noble or the most valiant person, in order to judge whether or not *The Cid* be a better play than *The Liberal Lover*.   I am not ' a man of explanations' (*d'éclaircissemens*), so that you are safe on that side." The warlike critic then betook himself to the new Academy, and solicited its judgment between the

Scuderi's cartel to Corneille, and Corneille's reply.

dramatist and the reviewer.   The Academicians were in no
haste to interfere.   They could foresee many phases to such
a contest, and some perils to their infant society. Chapelain
shared in the public admiration sufficiently to assure one of
his friends that he had lost a great treat in being absent
from the performance of *The Cid*, and to write to another
that, in his opinion, the subject, the ideas, and the embellishments, were alike deserving of the applause they had
received, although he "could not but deem the author
fortunate in not having to stand the test of *the more cultivated criticism of Italy.*"   It seems to have needed the
intervention of the Cardinal himself to obtain a formal
warrant for an Academic inquiry into the respective merits
of Corneille and his critics.

Why did
Richelieu
condemn *The
Cid?*
The aspersions which have been so lavishly cast on
almost all the events of Richelieu's career, are not lack-
ing even to this little incident.   Corneille had served on
that poetic staff with whose five members the Cardinal
was wont to work on his dramatic projects.   It is very
likely that the poet may have corrected the statesman's
rough drafts somewhat too freely.   But to infer that
Richelieu bore him malice on that score is gratuitous.
Unsupported by evidence, its probability is opposed by
what is known to have happened on a similar occasion.
The still more foolish story that Richelieu had offered
Corneille 100,000 crowns for the MS. of *The Cid*,—and
silence,—carries its own refutation.   Two aspects of that
famous tragedy, which are altogether independent of its
literary worth, might have served to explain Richelieu's dis-
taste, without any ascription of base motives.   It defended
duelling,* when the energies of the government were tasked

---

* In the verses which begin—
   "Les satisfactions n'apaisent point une ame," &c.

to put down a practice which had grown into a pestilence. It glorified Spain, when France had to struggle with her. Very easily may the critics of another age sever the intrinsic beauties of a play from the timeliness or untimeliness of its appearance, the merits or demerits of its personages, and the logical or illogical character of their arguments. But dates are important. The Englishman who should have thrown a poetic halo over Spanish heroes, just at the moment when other Englishmen were arming against a Spanish fleet, would scarcely, I think, have found an audience so impartial as that which greeted *The Cid* with tumultuous applause, in the 'year of Corbie,' as 1636 was significantly called.

However this may have been, the Cardinal's wishes were now known. The chief obstacle in the way of their gratification lay in that clause of the statutes which forbade the Academy from sitting in judgment on any works not submitted to it by their author. Possibly this proviso may have been inserted expressly with a view to the pending controversy. Corneille's consent was therefore indispensable. Boisrobert plied him with both arguments and entreaties ; in reply to which he obtained only excuses, in the shape of compliments. The occupation, said Corneille, was unworthy of the Academy's dignity. Scudéri's pamphlet deserved no answer from him, and therefore could not deserve to occupy the time of the Academicians. Such an inquiry, too, would be a bad precedent, since it would give to the meanest writers the notion that directly any great work was produced, they were empowered to enter into a controversy with the author in presence of the French Academy. But, in June, 1637, when told that the Cardinal was very desirous that he should comply, he answered : "The Academicians may do

The course taken by Corneille.

2

as they please. Since you tell me that the Cardinal will
be very glad to see their opinion, and that it will amuse
His Eminence, I have nothing more to say."

Upon this small concession, the Academy appointed a
Committee for the examination of the play, and of Scudéri's
Observations, consisting of Chapelain, Bourzeys, and
Desmarets. Two months afterwards, Chapelain writes to
Balzac : "The task could not have been given to a man
less capable than I am of satisfying the public expectations.
. . . . What embarrasses me is that I am forced to
offend both great and small, the Court and the Town, and
myself too, in dealing with a subject which ought not to be
treated by us. There is nothing more odious, nothing
which a discreet man should more carefully avoid, than
publicly to find fault with a work for which either the
author's reputation or his good fortune has won general
approval." Corneille, on the other hand, assures Boisrobert that he is "looking with much impatience for the
Academy's opinion, that he may know what course to
take. Till then," he adds, with a sharp stroke of irony,
"I can only work with some misgiving, *and shall not know
how to employ words with certainty.*" When the criticism
was submitted to Richelieu, he approved of its substance,
but thought that it wanted the graces of style. "You
must," he said, "throw in a few handfuls of flowers."
This business of embellishment was entrusted to some
worthy members, who were so prodigal of their flowers as
to bury the argument beneath them, and to anger the
Cardinal. He sent to desire that some of the Academicians would attend him forthwith. When the audience
was given, he addressed himself more particularly to
Chapelain (who has left a curiously minute account of the
interview), and with so much animation as to seize him by

the button of his coat, " as one does unconsciously, when very earnestly bent on convincing an opponent." The result was that Chapelain had again to revise the whole. When the task was finally completed, the chief author was able to say with a good conscience, " I believe the doctrine to be sound, and, in my opinion, equity and moderation prevail throughout."

Les Sentiments de l'Académie Française sur la Tragédie du Cid accorded high praise to many portions of the work. The " irregularities " of the plot were pointed out, as, by Academicians, they could scarcely fail to be. But it was added that " even the learned ought to tolerate indulgently the irregularities of a work which would not have had the good fortune to please the multitude so highly, had it not possessed uncommon merits. The freshness and vehemence of its passion, the force and delicacy of many of its thoughts, and that inexpressible charm which is mingled even with its faults, have obtained for it high rank amongst French poems of its class. If its author does not owe *all* his reputation to his merit, neither does he owe it all to fortune. Nature has been sufficiently bountiful to him to excuse fortune for being prodigal." So moderate a judgment, of course, satisfied neither author nor critic. Scudéri, indeed, affected to thank the Academy, but the affectation was evident. Corneille did not attempt to conceal his dissatisfaction. Whilst the Academy had been deliberating, the controversy had spread. Pamphlets had come from the press in a shower. Under such circumstances, the great dramatist altered his views. Instead of standing coldly aloof, he sought the opportunity of defending his work in person before his judges, and resented its refusal. He then carried De Castro's play, with his own hands, to the Cardinal, that he might convince himself how

The publication of the 'Sentiments de l'Académie Française.'

The result of the controversy.

small were the obligations of the French *Cid* to the Spanish one. When the *Sentiments* appeared he left Paris, and for a time ceased to write. In January, 1639, Chapelain tells Balzac that "Scudéri has at least gained thus much by the quarrel, that Corneille has taken a disgust at his art. His vein seems to be exhausted. I have tried as much as I could to excite him to avenge himself, both on Scudéri *and on his protectress*, by creating some new *Cid*, which shall again win universal praises, and prove that beauty may be independent of art; but I cannot succeed. He talks only of rules, and of the answers he could have made to the Academicians, if he had not been afraid of offending the authorities (*les puissances*). He even puts Aristotle amongst the apocryphal authors, when he cannot adapt him to his own views." But the depression was only temporary. And if Boileau sought antithetical point rather than plain truth, when he said—

"Au *Cid* persécuté, *Cinna* doit sa naissance,"

it is at least probable that the time of rest, like the time of adversity, had its sweet uses. Corneille, however, never forgot the mortifications which this controversy had brought upon him. He never forgave Richelieu for the share he had taken in it. The Cardinal had liberally befriended him. He had removed the obstacles which impeded Corneille's marriage. He had accorded letters-patent of nobility to the poet's father. Trivial as such a grant looks beside the trophies which Corneille has won by his own intellect, there is evidence that by himself it had been highly prized. So little did it appear to the poet's friends that he had real cause of complaint against the Cardinal, that, when Richelieu died, we find one of them, Sarrau, expressing his hope that Corneille would testify his regret by writing something that should be worthy both of the author and the subject; and adding, " Many will have cause to regret him, but none more than you. Had he lived longer he would have crowned you with the wreath of Apollo. You have lost an illustrious eulogist of your works, although, in truth, you stand in no need of eulogy," &c.* The author of *The Cid* felt little inclination to undertake the task which his correspondent pressed upon him. His momentary feelings dictated the verses :—

> " Qu'on parle mal ou bien du fameux Cardinal,
> Ma prose ni mes vers n'en diront jamais rien ;
> Il m'a fait trop de bien pour en dire du mal,
> Il m'a fait trop de mal pour en dire du bien :"

and it would have been to his honour if his latent animosity had never led him to forget the self-imposed restraint. Scarcely was Lewis XIII dead, when his resentment against the Cardinal burst forth in verse. Describing the reign of the monarch—

> " Dont la seule bonté deplut aux bons François,"

he proceeds to say that, by his bad choice of a Minister,

> " L'ambition, l'orgueil, la haine, l'avarice,
> Armés de son pouvoir, nous donnèrent des lois."

This makes a sorry contrast with the dedicatory epistle prefixed to *Horace* three years earlier, or with the laudation contained in Corneille's discourse at his reception into the Academy, four years later.

* *Claudii Sarravii Epistolæ*, Ep. 49 (Araus. 1654, pp. 65, 66).

CHAPTER III.

THE EARLY ELECTIONS AND EXCLUSIONS.— PATRU.— BOSSUET.—MÉNAGE.—RACINE.—THE BATTLE OF THE ANCIENTS AND THE MODERNS.—THE EXPULSION OF THE ABBÉ DE SAINT PIERRE.—THE ACADEMIC IMPEDIMENTS AND ULTIMATE TRIUMPHS OF MONTESQUIEU AND VOLTAIRE.

WITH increased numbers came ceremony and routine. The first Academician who addressed a formal speech of thanks to his colleagues, on his reception, was Olivier Patru, who succeeded Porchères d'Arbaud, in 1640. The compliment pleased, and became a practice. For several years, these speeches were little more than common-place compliments, sometimes hyperbolical, but usually having at least the merit of brevity. Everybody came in for his modicum of praise. Patru himself, practised orator and cool-headed lawyer as he was, went the length of assuring his colleagues that "it is enough for one age to have seen forty persons of such eminent merit and virtue. So great an effort must needs have exhausted Nature." Patru had been elected at the cost of the Abbé d'Aubignac, who had eagerly sought admission. D'Aubignac avenged himself by repeated endeavours to obtain a charter from the King for the establishment of a second Academy. Far from sharing Patru's admiring conviction that Nature must needs

The reception speech of Olivier Patru.

The abortive attempt to create a rival Academy.

have exhausted her powers in giving birth to the existing forty, he assures the King that Paris can boast a thousand such, and that the "kingdom at large could raise an army of them." But in vain did he seek to draw His Majesty's attention to the fact that already he himself, and certain of his friends, had "carried on their conferences for two years, in mutual communication of their studies," and that without going so far as to allege that these conferences included men as nobly impassioned for good letters as any in the kingdom, they might, at least, assert themselves to be not unworthy cadets of the French Academy.* D'Aubignac's "*Académie des belles lettres*," so it was called, had to be content with its weekly meeting in the Abbé's lodgings, and with a public assembly once a month at the Hotel Matignon.

The pre-eminence in hyperbolical flattery—one episcopal example, which will claim notice presently, excepted—was attained by Scudéri, whom the Academy elected not long after its reception of the poet who had conferred on him an immortality so different from that which had dazzled his imagination. He began his speech thus :—" He, gentlemen, who conceived that the Roman Senate was composed entirely of kings, would doubtless have taken you for gods, having regard to the sublimity of your minds and the immortality of your works." When he came to eulogize Richelieu, he assured his auditors that " to speak of things simply as they are, all the figures of arithmetic are insufficient to express his greatness." But this did not satisfy him. After he had already sent his intended speech to the Secretary (in accordance with the rules), he wrote to request the insertion of an additional sentence to this effect :—" The

Scuderi's opinion of Academic genius.

---

* *Discours au Roy sur l'Establissement d'une seconde Académie dans la Ville de Paris, par Messire Hedelin, Abbé d'Aubignac.*

Academy may justly designate itself *porphyrogenetic*, since it was born in the purple of Cardinals, of Kings, and of Chancellors." Conrart's modesty, or his good nature, forbade him to comply with the request, so that the new member's discourse was shorn of part of its brilliancy.

The address of Bossuet, at his reception in 1671.
The custom of a formal reply on behalf of the Academy to the speech of the Academician-elect does not appear to have been established until the reception of Bossuet, in 1671. That prelate's speech is one of the first in which a specific subject is expressly though (in his case,) briefly treated. Taking for his theme the French language, its rapid variation, its capabilities, the means of developing and systematizing it, and the duties in that direction imposed on the Academy, the discourse itself became an illustration of its own argument. Charpentier, in replying for the Academy, dwelt on another theme, in a way which contrasts piquantly with the ordinary tenor of the Academical discourses of the first thirty years. "There prevails," he said, "in the great world, I know not what contagion of display and pride which is strangely antagonistic to the meekness of philosophy. . . . The court has its *populace* as well as the town. The purple sometimes covers mediocre or even base souls. The personal merit which finds its reward within . . . is something higher than grandeur or wealth." But the gay audience, which for almost two centuries has been accustomed to set in so brilliant a frame the sombre business of an academical reception, was not yet present to profit by the lay sermon of M. Charpentier. It was preached only to his colleagues.

At this time, the Academy still met in the Hotel Séguier. Charles Perrault, whose admission followed that of Bossuet, originated the proposition that the reception should be public. It was also at his suggestion that a double scrutiny

—first by names written on slips, and then by the usual
black and white balls—was substituted for simple ballot,
in the elections. The Academy received in 1672 a royal
grant of apartments in the Louvre ; and it was there
that the first public reception—that of Fléchier—was held,
in the following year.

Thus far, the choice of new members had been made The reject-
from time to time with little dissension or scandal. The ed candidates —Ménage
most conspicuous of the unsuccessful candidates was and Queen Christina's
Ménage. When Christina of Sweden visited the Academy inquiry about him.
in 1658, her first question was, " Why is M. Ménage not
here ?" To which Boisrobert replied that certainly his
literary merits entitled him to a seat, but that his conduct
had made him unworthy of it. Perhaps, both his good and
his bad qualities would have rendered him a troublesome
member. His easy disposition made him, like Chapelain,
a man of many friends, and his quick resentments, a man
of many quarrels. When Christina herself had given him
permission to introduce to her any " men of merit " of his
acquaintance, her audience-chamber became so thronged
that she exclaimed, " This M. Ménage must know a marvellous number of people of merit." His *Requête des
Dictionnaires* bitterly offended many of the Academicians.
Habert de Montmor tried to persuade his colleagues that
the very assault was a reason for admission—" on the
principle which disposes people to compel a rake to marry
the girl whose fair fame has suffered from him." Long
afterwards, when Ménage was drawing near his end, it was
intimated to him that opposition had ceased, and that a
new candidature would be successful. " No," said he, " it
would now be a marriage *in extremis*, little to the credit
of either of us."

The first occasion on which the new member undertook
that review of the career and productions of his immediate
predecessor which has become so characteristic a feature of
the receptions, was a notable one.   Racine presided at the
admission (January, 1685) of two Academicians—Bergeret,
in the place of Cordemoy; and Thomas Corneille, in the
place of Pierre Corneille.   Bergeret gave a brief account of
the works and character of the Academician whose place
he was called to fill.   Thomas Corneille restricted himself,
on this head, to the few and simple words which became
so near a relative.   The speech of the day was that of
Racine.   Rising beyond the sphere of that petty malice
which had tried to make praises of Corneille turn to his own
disparagement, and anticipating comparisons between
"ancients and moderns" which were about to become a
war-cry among the writers and critics of France, and to
raise its echo amongst ourselves, he claimed for Corneille
an equal rank with Æschylus and Sophocles; and he
bore his testimony to that modesty of demeanour towards
his colleagues which made the author of *Cinna* " leave his
laurels at the Academy's door," and take an unobtrusive
share in the debates, even when they turned on dramatic
questions.

The war of
the Ancients
and the
Moderns.   The literary strife which led to the production of the
Parallèle des Anciens et des Modernes and its tribe of
followers, seems to have had its origin in an Academic
discussion between Racine and Perrault, some two years
after the reception of Thomas Corneille—in which, as we
have seen, Racine himself had no hesitation to place a contemporary on a level with the tragic poets of Greece.   He
now ironically complimented Perrault on the ingenuity
with which in his *Siècle de Louis XIV* he had sought to
raise above the ancients contemporaries of a calibre quite

unlike that of Corneille, and he coupled with the compliment a remark that it was not likely that the paradox would deceive anybody. Perrault was piqued into an elaborate exaggeration of his flattering estimate of the writers of the day, the best of whom, after all, he was least able to appreciate. Thus it happened that a contest, trivial in itself, was entered upon at a needless disadvantage. To institute a comparison between the greatest writers of all antiquity, and the Chapelains, the Scudéris, and the Saint Amants, of the seventeenth century, was so ludicrous that ere long Fontenelle, the only man of eminence who had supported Perrault, made his escape. " I," said he, " do not belong to the party which claims me for its chief."

The brunt of the battle lay between Perrault and Boileau. But La Bruyère dealt a few vigorous strokes for the honour of the ancients, and it chanced that he was elected an Academician whilst the paper war was still raging. In his address he drew some neat comparisons between men in whom the Academy had real cause to glory, and certain of the Roman poets, but pushed the question no further. Charpentier replied, and took occasion to extend the ground, and to give it anything rather than a literary turn :—
" Not to speak of the thousand admirable inventions which have been discovered within the last two hundred years," "let us look," he said, " at the things which lie at this moment before our eyes. This magnificent building of *The Louvre*—is it not as fine as the most superb edifice of the ancients ? Is not the art of war as well understood now as then ? Are the sieges of Luxembourg, of Mons, and Namur, less remarkable than those of Tyre, Saguntum, or Carthage ? And, as to eloquence, if its object be to please, to carry the mind away captive, and if it be also true—as we know by daily experience—that our orators

Perrault and
Boileau.

do really attain those ends, it is useless to question whether
or not they are eloquent, still more useless to dispute
whether their eloquence is greater or less than that of the
ancients. For my part, I would as lief ask if the sea is as
salt now, as it was in the time of the Roman Republic."

On the death of Perrault, his seat was sought by the
Abbé Chaulieu, a consummate specimen of that epicurean
section of the French clergy which so long kept its ground
beside the Fenelons and the Bourdaloues, redeeming the
time not abandoned to sloth by epigrams and anacreontic
verses. Some of the shafts of Chaulieu's wit had pierced
Tourreil, who, when the vacancy occurred, happened to be
Director. He resolved to defeat his assailant by assuring
the Academicians that the President de Lamoignon would
feel honoured by their suffrages. The President was
elected, but he disavowed his proposer, and declined the
seat. The Academy then made a bye-law that the preliminary visits of a candidate, which, theretofore, had been
usual but not obligatory, should for the future be exacted.
Armand de Rohan, Prince Bishop of Strasburg, was elected
in Perrault's stead.

Few of the gaudy days of the French Academy have
offered a more attractive entertainment to the Parisian
loungers than did the reception, in 1694, of François de
Clermont Tonnerre, Bishop of Noyon, the prelate of whose
excessive vanity Saint Simon has given us so curious a
picture. Elected partly as one of those decorative members
who served to link the Academy with the Court, and
partly, it is to be feared, by way of malicious sport, he
determined to do honour to the occasion by a most elaborate discourse, which bristles with the great names of
universal history. Moses and Constantine, Tertullian and
Solomon, Alexander the Great and St. Ambrose, are

The recep-
tion in 1694,
of the courtly
Bishop of
Noyon.

mixed pell-mell in an oration which is doubtless unique. After exhausting eulogy in praise of "Lewis, so amiable for the charms of his person," and of " Lewis, so admirable for the greatness of his reign," he implored his colleagues " not to wonder at the zeal of this discourse. Every phrase is a tongue of flame; mouth and heart are in unison. And it would be easy to justify them by the example of Gregory Nazianzen, insatiable in the praises of St. Basil the Great." The reply of the Abbé de Caumartin was a masterpiece of dexterous satire, each shaft of which took effect on every auditor save one. The poor bishop, however, listened, without a moment's misgiving, to the assurance that "whilst the church sees in your episcopal charges sound doctrine and pure morality, we Academicians see, also, elegant allusions, well-sustained allegories, and a methodic arrangement, not elsewhere to be found, without which it would be difficult to follow ideas so magnificent as yours." The good-hearted prelate, it is said, had no conception of the emotions which must have so severely tested the polished demeanour of that gay assembly, until he found, a day or two afterwards, that his reception had become the table-talk of the town. Even then, his anger was but momentary. He was as proud as ever of his Academical dignity, and even sought opportunities to promote the interests of his colleagues.

At this period, the Academicians whose careers, however distinguished, were not literary, and the merely court-members, had become so numerous as to induce dissatisfaction among some of the workers. D'Olivet, the second of the Academy's historians, assigns, as one of his reasons for refusing to comply with the request that he would carry his narrative beyond 1699, the fact that " the number of noblemen and prelates has increased in our society. Now, with a few exceptions, there is no pleasure in writing about them. One is sure to offend their families unless one narrates everything they did, however little connected with Academical pursuits." On the other hand, it is just to bear in mind that certain really great names of the period we have been glancing at—names whose absence from the roll is now so salient—rarely, if ever, indicate exclusions in favour of courtiers, soldiers, or prelates. One of the Academy's rules, established not very long after the foundation—and, whether wise or unwise, certainly not personal—made residence near Paris a necessary qualification. Descartes, Rotrou, Regnard, were usually remote from the capital, and thus by rule ineligible. Antoine Arnauld—

The men who were kept out.

> "Le plus savant mortel qui jamais ait écrit,"—

is said to have refused a seat, after it had been proffered to him. La Rochefoucauld also stood aloof by choice. The exclusion of Pascal, Malebranche, and Molière depended on other powers, royal or social, not on the Academy. Had Richelieu lived a little longer, it is probable that one social disqualification, at all events, would have been removed. But of all the men thus excluded, the Academy might have said, as it actually said of one of them on a memorable occasion :—

> "Rien ne manque à leur gloire ; ils manquaient à la notre."

Other men of humbler rank in the literary hierarchy, but superior in point of talent to many Academicians, have been excluded, sometimes by considerations—irrespective of talent—which no Society has the right to overlook, as in the instance of Dufresnoy ; sometimes by the combination of imprudence with misrepresentation, such as time only could fully dispel, as in that of Jean Baptiste Rousseau.

The case last named is a notable one. Those bitterly

satirical couplets which Rousseau had so recklessly flung about him in his youth were surreptitiously collected and reprinted when their author sought a seat in the Academy. The anonymous collector was base enough to forge additional verses, still more offensive than the real ones, and such as were sure to increase animosity in quarters where the poet had most cause to dread it.   Discovering that a certain Academician had helped to circulate these verses, he rashly charged him with the forgery, in the absence of all evidence.   The controversy became envenomed, and eventually Rousseau found himself condemned by a decree of Parliament to perpetual exile.   This was in April, 1712. Four years afterwards, letters of recall were obtained, but he refused to avail himself of them, insisting on his right to a full acquittal.   Twenty-two years more were passed in irksome banishment, sometimes at Brussels, sometimes in other parts of the Netherlands.   His exile was occasionally—but not always happily—enlivened by visits from comrades in literature.   At one such visit, Rousseau read to Voltaire his *Ode to Posterity*.   " I am afraid, my friend," observed his caustic auditor, " that that letter will never reach its address."   At length, Rousseau sought, but without success, to obtain the favour he had formerly refused. He ventured to visit Paris, furtively, and then returned to Brussels to die.

It would be easy to point to other cases in which candidates were opposed from discreditable motives ; sometimes from petty jealousies and personal dislikes ; at other times from that spirit of coterie which is the especial bane of corporations, whether learned or unlearned.   Any impartial survey, however, of the history of the French Academy must, I think, result in the conviction that the exercise of

Jean Bapt. Rousseau— reason of his exclusion.

the power it has really possessed has, in the main, been independent and honourable. The war between the privileged
few within, and the wits without, is too amusing a resource
to be suffered to die for want of ammunition.   But the
most satirical of the lampooners, on the wrong side of the
door, have sometimes lived long enough to become lam-
pooned Academicians, seated on comfortable cushions, in
their turn.   The cool sagacity which prompted Fontenelle
—"his heart all brains, like his head"—to address to the
Academy, after five defeats, a polished *Discourse on Patience*,
is not vouchsafed to every man.

The charac-
ter, the pro-
jects, and the
Academic dis-
grace of St.
Pierre.

The worst blot on the Academy's escutcheon is its expulsion of the Abbé de Saint Pierre. That was a dastardly,
but, happily for its fame, an exceptional deed.   As an
Academician, Saint Pierre had distinguished himself by
his zealous exertions to make the society both more powerful and more useful.   He strove to obtain the substitution,
on its public days, of appreciations of the lives and works
of the great men of France, for insipid disquisitions on
"the inconveniences of wealth," or "the advantages of a
good reputation."   Remembering what sort of reading had
first stirred his own youthful pulses to a lofty and pure
ambition, he was eager to make the recollection fruitful
for the youth to come.   He also strove for a re-modelling
of the Academy, with a view to systematic division of
labour, which, in some respects, anticipated part of Napoleon's ultimate organization of the Institute.   Saint Pierre's
whole life, indeed, was an anticipation.   The Cardinals
Dubois, and the Regent Dukes of that day, might very
naturally call his projects of political and social reform
"a good man's dreams," but he himself might have said,
with Schiller's Marquis Posa—

" Das Jahrhundert
Ist meinem Ideal nicht reif. Ich lebe
Ein Burger derer welche kommen werden."

Saint Pierre's offence consisted in an honest and outspoken condemnation of some of the base acts of the
Government of Lewis XIV, and especially in his strong
censure of that adulation of the King himself, which found
almost daily expression in the epithet " Lewis the Great."
In a certain *Discours sur la Polysynodie*, he had taken
occasion to say, in words which deserve to be remembered,
" We may well call him ' Lewis the Powerful,' or, ' Lewis
the Terrible,' for none of his predecessors was so powerful;
none made himself so terrible.   But those who possess
even moderate discrimination will never call him ' Lewis
the Great ;' will never confound power with true greatness.
For great power, unless it has been employed in procuring
great benefits for mankind in general, and for its subjects
and neighbours in particular, will never make a man esti-
mable.   In a word, great power alone will never make a
great man."

The attack upon Saint Pierre was led by the Cardinal
de Polignac.   At that time, courtiers and prelates were in
unusual force in the Academy.   The sitting (April, 1718)
was a very stormy one.   Another Cardinal (Fleury, then
Chancellor of the Academy) strongly condemned the incriminated passages, and artfully contrived to give a sort
of complexion of generosity to the proposed censure, by
reminding the Academicians that the monarch whose fame
had been assailed by their fellow-member was dead, and a
benefactor.   Should it be said of them that they were so
venal, so wholly given up to selfish interests, that their
eulogies lasted exactly as long as their patron was living
and powerful?   Then, and afterwards, Saint Pierre vainly

3

tried to be heard in his defence. He was expelled. His place was not filled up. On his death, he was allowed a funeral service, but was refused the customary biographical honours at the reception of his successor. Not until 1775 was this additional stigma on the Academy removed. But no occasion could have been more fitting for the rehabilitation of Saint Pierre's memory than was the reception of Malesherbes.

Saint Pierre's expulsion may be regarded as the first of a long series of incidents in the quarrel of "philosophers" and "anti-philosophers," in which the Academic strife did but reflect what was passing in other and larger spheres of French life, and is therefore very interesting to students of history, but most of which must here be passed over in silence. The contests, however, about the election, first of Montesquieu, and afterwards of Voltaire, claim some notice.

The candidature of Montesquieu. Montesquieu offered himself as candidate for a seat which was vacated in 1727. In the *Lettres Persanes* he had criticised the reign of Lewis XIV with a severity far keener than Saint Pierre's. But it was easier to suppress, for the time, a score of such men as the amiable author of the *Discours sur la Polysynodie*, than to cope with one Montesquieu. The great thinker who was to open the way for such momentous changes in the social polity of France, was also the pet author of his day. Everybody read and quoted him. The booksellers ran about imploring all their acquaintances to write them some *Lettres Persanes*, as though to write *Lettres Persanes* had been as easy as to sell them. Unhappily, there were in this famous book some sarcasms on religion which the author's own later and better thoughts condemned. His enemies were quick to seize their advantage. The Academy was officially informed that the King would not confirm its choice, should that choice fall on the author of the incriminated book.   Montesquieu resented this interference by declaring that, if the threatened prohibition were enforced, he would seek in a foreign land the protection and the honours denied him in his own.   Another step which he is said to have taken, in this conjuncture, has been very differently described.

According to Voltaire's version of the affair, Montesquieu caused his book to be rapidly reprinted, with the omission of the obnoxious passages, and without any mention of the alterations he had made.   He then in person carried the book to the Minister.   D'Alembert repeats this account, substantially, but asserts that the passages suppressed were really spurious.   Another contemporary writer names two persons who shared, he says, in the authorship of the book, in its original and anonymous form.   But he throws no spark of light on the then curious phenomenon that the work of three authors should bear, so strikingly, the impress of one mind.   Montesquieu's more recent biographers, on the other hand, deny the story altogether. Whatever may have been the precise incidents, it is certain that there are portions of the *Persian Letters* which their author, himself, condemned, as his mere *juvenilia*, and nobly atoned for in his later writings.   It is also certain that the obstacle to his election was removed in an honourable way.   The man who, with his dying breath, said in reference to this very book: "I will yield everything to Religion, but nothing to the Jesuits," was not the man to win his seat in the Academy by a mere subterfuge.

Voltaire, in his turn, had to fight his way.   He offered himself as the successor of Cardinal de Fleury.   At first, *The struggle and ultimate triumph of Voltaire.*

it was found not very easy to obtain a presentable opponent.
But Boyer, Bishop of Mirepoix, who had long played the
part of Cerberus at the Academy's door, was indefatigable
in his efforts. Witticisms rained upon him, until the poor
prelate at last made formal complaint to the king that " M.
de Voltaire made him pass for a fool, even at foreign
courts," and had to put up with a new sarcasm, from the
royal lips. But he had the satisfaction of keeping Voltaire
out until 1746.

At this time, Voltaire had not yet reached those final
cross-roads which present themselves, alike to the men of
books and to the men of action, at a certain stage in their
career—when the upward or the downward course comes
to be fixed for ever. He had already published *La Hen-
riade*—after once casting it into the fire, in his hot impatience of outspoken criticism—together with *Zaire*,
Mérope, the *Lettres Anglaises*, and the *Vie de Charles XII.*
In addition to his marvellous talent and versatility, he had
displayed only too much of his thin sciolism, of his morbid
vanity, and of his angry "philosophy." But his better
Angel had not yet given him over to that evil genius who
was soon afterwards to inspire the wretched sophistries,
and the puerile credulities, of the *Dictionnaire Philoso-
phique;* the scarcely sane egotism of the *Correspondance
avec d'Alembert;* and the scarcely human crapulousness of
La Pucelle. The man whom prelates and courtiers were
now unscrupulously opposing had, indeed, already exhibited
the shallowness as well as the brilliancy of his intellect.
But he had not yet openly committed himself to the task
of overthrowing Christianity, by dint of scurrilous jests
and puny diatribes. He was already a profane scoffer,
and a sceptical bigot. He was *not*, as yet, the mere Vitru-
vius of ruin. Only at a somewhat later period in his

career was he, in the happy words of Byron, to multiply himself among mankind—

> "The Proteus of their talents; whilst his own
> Breathed most in ridicule; which, as the wind,
> Blew where it listed, laying all things prone,
> Now to o'erthrow a fool, and now to shake a throne."

When he presented himself at the Academy's door, he stood on ground which he had cultivated usefully, and had fairly made his own. If literary ability was ever to win the literary laurel, his pretensions were just.

In Voltaire's hands the customary Academical eulogies were cut short. He dwelt, at his reception, on the growth of the language and the literature of France, making small account of all writers antecedent to Corneille. Those are not truly good books, he said, which do not pass the frontiers. Before Corneille, the only author who had attracted the attention of the few foreigners conversant with French was Montaigne; and long after Marot, the language, even to Frenchmen, was but a domestic jargon, enlivened by a few pleasantries. Corneille was the first to make it respected abroad, and he did this just at the time that Richelieu was beginning to win respect for the crown. Both, together, spread the fame of France over Europe. After Corneille come, not indeed great geniuses, but better writers.

CHAPTER IV.

BUFFON AND THE COURTIER PARADIS DE MONCRIF.—THE WAR OF ADMINISTRATORS AND ACADEMICIANS.—COURT DISGRACE OF THE RHETORICIAN THOMAS.—CHAMFORT AND MIRABEAU.—THE ACADEMY DISSOLVED.

SEVEN years later, Buffon followed Voltaire's lead by an address, pithy and luminous, on "style;" which became authoritative. He showed what should be the aim of an ambitious writer, and how it should be pursued. He hit blots in the common methods of education, which are neither peculiar to France, nor defunct with the eighteenth century. A tolerable ear, he says, suffices for the avoidance of dissonant words; the reading of poets and orators, for a mechanical imitation of poetical cadence, or of rhetorical artifice. But imitation is never creative. Ideas must precede sentences. What is to be written should be first wrought out clearly in thought. Everything which is merely ornamental and redundant should be looked at with distrust. These are among the counsels which the author of the *Histoire Naturelle* gives to those who seek distinction by the pen, and they have lost nothing in point or relevancy.

Buffon on literary style.

It chanced that the courtier Paradis de Moncrif presided at this reception. Of him it was said that, at Versailles, he was a devotee; at Paris, a man of pleasure. On this occasion, he seems to have brought his courtly devotion to town with him, and to have given it a very unseasonable airing. The Doctors of the Sorbonne had just attacked both Montesquieu and Buffon, and the attacks had recoiled. Moncrif dragged into his official reply a very superfluous eulogy of those venerable doctors. There was then no opportunity of rejoinder. But, immediately afterwards, the publication of a new volume of his great work enabled Buffon to give to the public—in two letters written by the Sorbonne theologians themselves—consummate examples of the "style" which should be detested. Montesquieu, on his part, in the *Défense de l'Esprit des Lois*, gave himself the satisfaction, not so much of overthrowing his assailants, as of making them glide softly to the ground, amidst the laughter of the bystanders.

Buffon's revenge on the courtly parasites.

The war thus so repeatedly forced within the walls of the Academy between Past and Future—between the old generation, so reluctant to admit that one phase, at least, of its work is over, and the new generation, so eager to confound, in undiscriminating onslaught, what is really effete in the world with what is merely diseased—was diversified by many incidents, often ludicrous, sometimes tragic. The inevitable Mirepoix brought on the Academy a flood of epigrams (but no "*Discours sur la Patience*"), by his obstinate hostility to the election of Piron. Epigrams were lavished, too, on one of the new members, the poor Count of Clermont, resulting in the violent death of an unlucky epigrammatist, and in the verification of one of his sarcasms* in an unexpected fashion. The noble Academician never again

Piron—"qui ne fuit rieu."

---

* Trente-neuf joints à zéro,
  Si j'entend bien mon numero,
  N'ont jamais pu faire quarante.
  D'où je conclus, troupe savante,
  Qu'ayant à vos côtés admis
  Clermont, cette masse pesante,
  Ce digne cousin de Louis,
  La place est encore vacante.

appeared amongst his colleagues.   In like manner, the
notorious Le Franc de Pompignan—one of the many
assailants of the "Philosophers" who entirely failed to
fasten on those amongst their characteristics which were
most reprehensible, and which made the name a palpable
misnomer—was so completely immolated with the meal
and salt of the satirists, that he forsook Paris, and passed
almost a quarter of a century in seclusion.   Meanwhile,
that growing influence of the men of letters on Society
which every passing day made more unmistakeably evident,
was scornfully ignored by the ostensible rulers of France.
Its very mention within the walls of a literary society was
treated as a crime.

The minis-
terial attacks
and censure
on Thomas.
Thomas, a man of real ability, but whose rhetoric was
wont to run away with his discretion, had drawn in an
Academical oration of 1767 a highly-coloured picture of
that "quiet study in which the man of letters sits, meditat-
ing, and summons before him Justice and Humanity,"
and so on.   Then, that magnification of the literary office
was thought rather ludicrous, but not dangerous.   Three
years afterwards, and with somewhat better taste, he pursued the same theme in an "*Eloge de Marc Aurèle.*"   By
the public, this eulogy was rapturously applauded; by the
Government, it was instantly suppressed.   A few days later,
when officiating as president at the reception of the Archbishop of Toulouse, Thomas dwelt, with all his force, upon
the reciprocal duties of thinkers and of statesmen, and upon
the necessity of harmonising action with opinion. This time,
the MS. was seized, and the orator silenced.   He was
forbidden to speak in the Academy, and was threatened
with severer penalties if any portion of that discourse should
appear in print or be circulated in manuscript.   But such
topics continued to be treated by other minds, and to be

encountered by like repression. This persistent attempt to crush effects by the easy process of ignoring causes, receives curious illustration when we find the great literary news-writer of the day, after narrating these occurrences, asking —not in irony, but in grave sincerity—"How is it possible that men of letters can be seditious, when they are never permitted to meddle with public affairs? In what country, in what age, has literature ever been regarded as a social function?"*

In the course of this conflict, the old Censorship of essays was re-established. On one occasion, the censors cut out a passage, condemnatory of the Inquisition, from an eulogy of Charles V of France.† The crowning incident in the long struggle was the suppression of La Harpe's *Eulogy of Fenelon.* It was, surely, in fit sequence that the illustrious prelate whom Lewis XIV had vainly tried to disgrace, should be hateful to such a successor and to such a court. This suppression was followed up by a royal letter, which impressed on the Academicians their duty to make a *discreet* choice in filling up vacancies; named, with praise, two Academicians whose "wisdom and moderation" had merited royal pensions; and announced his Majesty's gracious willingness to grant similar rewards to such of their colleagues "as should emulate their virtues." But there were no new candidates for venal pensions. One, at least, of the two favoured Academicians felt shame at the praises of Lewis XV, and, despite all precautions, unpalatable truths still found utterance from Academic benches.

In 1776, the Academy won, from its exiled member at Ferney, a compliment very little to its credit. "D'Alembert and our other friends," wrote Voltaire to La Harpe, "are

The suppression of the Eulogy of Fenelon.

---

* Grimm and Diderot, *Correspondance littéraire*, viii, 388.
† Voltaire, *Correspondance*, 15 August, 1776.

doing a patriotic work in daring to defend in the Academy Sophocles, Corneille, Euripides, and Racine, against Gilles, Shakespeare, and Pierrot le Tourneur." Le Tourneur had dared to call Shakespeare the "Divinity of the Stage;" "the highest type of true tragic art." But, after all, it is from the vile pen of an English scribbler that Voltaire borrows his closing taunt: "Rymer," he says, "had good ground to assert that Shakespeare ' was a wretched ape.' "*

During the reign of Lewis XVI the most notable receptions were those of Malesherbes (1775), La Harpe (1776), Ducis (1779), Chamfort (1781), and Target (1785). **The career of Chamfort.** Chamfort had been nursed in the Academy's lap. While yet "young, poor, and proud" (as Grimm describes him, in August, 1764), he obtained a poetry prize for his *Épître d'un père à son fils*, which was followed by several other like successes. When received as an Academician, he eulogised that chivalrous old France of which his predecessor, Saint Palaye, had been so enamoured, but with a warmth of colouring of which Saint Palaye was incapable. Broad, indeed, is the contrast between this discourse and the flimsy diatribe in which Chamfort, in the early days of the Revolution, attacked his foster-mother as " useless, ridiculous, despicable, and degraded; " given over to " servility," and shamefully implicated in " that most infamous of trades, the traffic in the liberties of nations."

At that time, violent abuse—if copious enough—went far towards supplying the most pitiable lack of argument. And Chamfort's mind had already lost its balance. He has himself somewhere said—speaking of his own sensual passions—" I have destroyed them, as a furious rider kills

* Voltaire and D'Alembert, *Correspondance*, 7 Oct., 1771. [Edition of 1837, x, 705.]

his horse." But he had really destroyed something higher and nobler. Chateaubriand scarcely needed to express his amazement that one who had so large a knowledge of mankind, should yet be so fierce a partisan. It is as easy to emasculate, by vicious indulgence, the mind, as the body. Chamfort was of that unhappy temper which had rather rule in hell, than serve in heaven. Truth and falsehood, to a mind of that strain, vary with the impressions of the passing hour. At first, an impetuous promoter of the Revolution, at all hazards, he at length tried to guide it; and when he found it too strong for him, he assailed it with the utmost bitterness. He tried to rule the French Academy, and failing to achieve even that, he sought its destruction. He knew that the primary functions of the Academy made it, implicitly, an antagonist of despotism. He knew that it had powerfully aided in raising the literary profession to responsibility and comparative independence. He knew that some of the best minds in France had been proud of its fellowship. The internecine war which had been waged between the Academy and the corrupt ministries of Lewis XV was within his own memory. Its history had been the theme of his own warm and repeated praises. But when he praised it, he had eyes only for the bright side of a long and varied career. When he vilified it, he could see nothing save the dark spots.

Character of Chamfort.

His attack on the Academy.

Accusation, in revolutionary times, is often but another word for doom. It was planned that a second denunciation, also written by Chamfort, should be uttered in the National Assembly by Mirabeau, who, but a few years before, had used very different language in supporting the pretensions of Target to a seat. Mirabeau's death intervened, but the Academy's fall was not long delayed, and it carried with it that of all similar corporations throughout France. The

The dissolution of the Academy.

seal of the Republic was affixed to its doors in August, 1793. The foresight of Morellet, then secretary, had, by a "pious larceny"—as he calls it in his *Memoirs*—previously secured the Charter, a nearly complete series of Minutes, and other MSS. Eighty portraits of Academicians were successfully concealed within the Louvre itself, until the dawn of better days. A decree, passed during the last throes of the Reign of Terror (July, 1794), declared the property of the suppressed Academies to be National property.

The "Constitution of the year III." decreed the creation of a National Institute "for the collection of discoveries and the improvement of the arts and sciences." Hence, eventually, arose the restored French Academy, but that restoration formed no part of the original design.

CHAPTER V.

THE ACADEMIC PRIZES AND THEIR RESULTS, UP TO THE
DATE OF THE REVOLUTIONARY DISSOLUTION.—CREATION
AND SUBSEQUENT REORGANIZATION OF THE INSTITUTE.
—RETURN OF THE SURVIVING ACADEMICIANS.

THUS far I have sought to exhibit something of the
work and influence of this remarkable institution, chiefly
by noticing the more conspicuous among the men who
received its honours, the themes chosen for its public displays, and its attitude towards the government of the day.
I have yet to mention the " prizes " which it either established or administered.   Of another and very prominent
function—the preparation of the *Dictionnaire de l'Académie
Française*—nothing can here be said.   Few books have a
more curious history, but to treat it fairly would require
time and space not now available.   I indulge the hope of
writing something on that subject hereafter.

Balzac, as early as the year 1655, established the
" Eloquence prize," the themes of which were, for a long
time, limited to religion and ethics.   Saint Pierre's unsuccessful suggestion, that it should be given to biographical
eulogies of the great men of France, was revived, with
better fortune, by Duclos, in 1758.   Before this date, the
laureated names are, Colin, Roy, Ragon, Nicolas, and the
like.   After it, we find Thomas, La Harpe, Necker, Garat,
Lacretelle, De Gerando, Fabre, Villemain.   If another list
could be framed of those youthful minds to whom such

*Balzac's
eloquence
prize.*

brief and vigorous biographies of Fenelon, Montesquieu, Pascal, Malesherbes, have given a spur—

> To scorn delights and live laborious days,

we should probably have a very apposite vindication of the " utility " of the institution, in this department of its work. Nor is it the Academy's smallest merit that, whilst glorifying intellectual power, it has repeatedly testified to the due subordination of literature to life.

Paul Pellisson and the Poetry prize.

Paul Pellisson followed Balzac's example, by founding a " Poetry prize." His own verses are very poor, but much of his life is a worthy theme for poetry. His faithful service and adherence to Fouquet cost him a long imprisonment. In the Bastille he wrote those defences of his fallen master which are the best, as well as the best known, productions of his pen. There, too, he accomplished that musical education of a spider which has become so famous. When released, he made, for the rest of his life, the anniversary of his freedom, the liberation day of several poor prisoners. Madame de Sevigné might well say of him, that "although he abused the privilege men have to be ugly, a noble soul dwelt in that uncouth form." For one of these Pellisson prizes, Voltaire was an unsuccessful candidate. Sixty-five years afterwards, "Voltaire" was the theme of another. The last prize given before the suppression was the first triumph of Fontanes.

Creation of the French Institute.

The creation of the Institute, decreed in 1794, was not effected until nearly the close of 1795. It was to have 144 members, in three classes: I, Physical and Mathematical Sciences; II, Moral and Political Sciences; III, Literature and the Fine Arts. The ideas of the period are characteristically reflected in the apportionment of 126 members to Sciences and Arts, and of 18 members to Literature.   In April, 1796, the Institute was installed in the Louvre.   The Statutes had directed that the alternate sittings of each class should be public.   Within a fortnight of the installation, a new by-law was imposed on the Institute, which abrogated that proviso, because "too much publicity was attended rather with inconvenience than advantage."   It was significantly added, that "this new regulation shall not be printed."   Next year, five members of the Institute—Barthélemy, Carnot, Pastoret, Sicard, and Fontanes—were sentenced to be "deported" to Cayenne, and they were not restored to their seats until after Napoleon's triumph on the 18th of Brumaire.

At the end of 1802, the Institute ceased to retain the form which the Convention had assigned to it.   Proud as Napoleon was of its fellowship, and ostentatiously as he wore its uniform, he had never liked its organization.   In his eyes a "Class of Moral and Political Sciences" was open to two weighty objections.   At the best, it would be but an elaborate machine for wasting time in the discussion of "unprofitable theories."   If it chanced to fall under the lead of "wrong-headed men," it would turn into a sort of political opposition, likely to be none the less troublesome for wearing a mask.   The purely literary section of the Institute, he, at this time, regarded with greater complacency.   He once said, with that felicity of expression which, in his best moments, so often gave wings to his thoughts, "I love the sciences. Each of them is a beautiful application of a part of the human mind. But literature is the mind itself."   Napoleon never approved of the plans of that somewhat pretentious little circle to which his brother Lucien and his sister Eliza belonged, in conjunction with Suard, Morellet, and Fontanes, and in which the

Its reorganization by Napoleon.

restoration of the old Academy, unaltered, was advocated. But he was willing to give literature freer scope in the Institute, and anxious that the great task of the Dictionary should be vigorously prosecuted.

With these views, he re-organized the Institute in January, 1803. Four classes were assigned to it :—I, Physical and Mathematical Sciences ; II, French Language and Literature ; III, Ancient Languages and Literature ; IV, Fine Arts. The Class of Moral and Political Sciences was nominally merged in the Class of French Literature, but was, in fact, suppressed. "A Class of Literature," said Napoleon, on this occasion, "must needs be trivial, and a 'Class of Moral Sciences' pedantic, if they can be really separated. Writers who are not thinkers, and thinkers who are not writers, will soon cease to be either the one or the other." To the budding Emperor, a better argument would have been less convenient. The "Forty" of the old Academy was to be the number of the new literature class, and its survivors—with one exception— were to resume their seats. The total number of members of the Institute was raised to 165.

The return of the survivors of the old Academy. Among the surviving Academicians, the names of La Harpe, Suard, Ducis, Target, St. Lambert, and Delille, are conspicuous. One of them, the Count of Bissy, had been an Academician in 1750. The new members included Volney, Garat, Cambacérès, Cabanis, Bernardin de Saint Pierre, Sièyes, Merlin, Rœderer, Fontanes, Ségur, Portalis, Marie Joseph Chénier, with others of less note. The most prominent of the subsequent elections, during the reign of Napoleon, were those of Maury, of Destutt de Tracy, and of Chateaubriand.

Cardinal Maury was the only survivor of the "Forty" who had been excluded from the Institute at its reorgani-

zation. He was then among the zealous enemies of Napoleon. But the hoped-for reverses in the Emperor's
fortunes tarried, and Maury's ardour cooled. Growing
weary of his long exile at Montefiascone, he at length
wrote to Napoleon, and obtained an interview at Genoa.
In 1806, he was permitted to return, and in 1807 was
elected into the Institute to fill the place of Target, who·
had been his junior in the old Academy.

Maury's reputation drew a large audience to his reception. He was known to be an orator as well as a wit.
Curiosity was heightened by the singularity of the circumstances. A man who had taken his seat in the Academy
as successor, under Lewis XV, of the unlucky and still
unforgotten Le Franc de Pompignan, was now, under
Napoleon, to biographize Target, whose weaknesses he was
thought little likely to spare. The excitement which prevailed
in certain circles is curiously shown, by the fact that Target's
admirers had a vindication of him (especially in relation to
his refusal to plead for Lewis XVI at the bar of the Convention), printed beforehand, and distributed at the doors
of the Academy. But the precaution was needless, and
the public disappointment great. The Cardinal injured
no reputation save his own. Avoiding Target, he took for
his theme a certain Abbé de Radonvilliers—who had died
uneulogized, during the Academy's suspension—the dullness of whose career quite overpowered Maury's own
vivacity. All that his ill-willers felt to be necessary for
the gratification of their spite, was the circulation, in the
newspapers,—amongst the Parisian occurrences of the day
—of the announcement that " On the 6th instant, an eminent personage drowned himself, not far from the Pont-des
Arts."

CHAPTER VI.

Scottish
origin of De
Tracy.

ANTOINE Louis Claude Destutt de Tracy was the eldest son of Claude Charles Louis Destutt de Tracy, Marquis of Tracy, and a Peer of France, and of Marie Emilie de Verzure. He was born on the 20th of July, 1754. Descended as he was from a long line of distinguished soldiers —the founder of whom had come to France, from Scotland, with John Stewart, Earl of Buchan, and, like him (although without winning, as Buchan won, the leading-staff of a Marshal of France), fought with distinction on behalf of Charles VII—he entered the army at an early age, and in 1776 had already attained the rank of Lieutenant-Colonel in the Royal Regiment of Horse. In 1788, he took an active part in the proceedings of the Provincial States of the Bourbonnais; was elected by the nobility of that province a member of the States General, and distinguished himself in the Constituent Assembly by his labours on questions of educational and social reform. With Lafayette, he served on the frontier, as commander-in-chief of the cavalry; and when that general left his army, De Tracy too retired to Auteuil, where he exchanged the life of a legislator and a soldier for that of a student.

At the outset, his attention was chiefly bestowed on the

physical sciences, and especially on chemistry. During the Reign of Terror, he was dragged from his retirement, and confined in the Carmelite Prison.   Here he read Locke and Condillac; meditated deeply on the processes of his own mind; and, on a memorable day, the 23rd of July, 1794 (5 Thermidor, year II), whilst the dismal corridors of the old monastery were echoing with the long roll-call for the guillotine, in which he had reason to expect that at any moment he might hear his own name, he marked the outlines and wrote down the main propositions of that system of "Ideology," which it was to be the grand aim of his unexpectedly prolonged life to embody in detail.   Four days afterwards, Robespierre fell, but many months elapsed before De Tracy could return to his home.

At Auteuil, the fascinating widow of Helvetius was long the centre of a brilliant circle, in which the philosophers of the day played no unimportant part.   Siéyès, Volney, Garat, Cabanis, De Tracy, met there habitually.   The two last named were soon linked in close friendship.   Together, they became members of the newly founded National Institute, at whose meetings the dissertations in which De Tracy first gave to the world his views of ideology, alternated with those in which Cabanis worked out, physiologically, the famous theory of Condillac, that all our intellectual operations, whether passive or active, are but transformed sensations.

An eminent historian of recent philosophy in France has characterized and discriminated the respective labours of the three most eminent members of this Auteuil circle, by calling Cabanis, the physiologist; Volney, the moralist; and De Tracy, the metaphysician, of the sensational school.*

* Damiron. *Histoire de la Philosophie en France au XIX* *Siècle*. i, 109.

To marshal into rigid order, our "means of knowing," to elicit the laws which govern, and the secret links which connect, the formation, the expression, and the deduction of our ideas, was the task which De Tracy had in the Carmelite Prison marked out for himself, or for his unknown successor. "Ideology is a branch of Zoology;" "to think is to feel;" such are the epigrammatic axioms in which he expresses his characteristic thoughts.

The Elements of Ideology.

According to De Tracy, our intellectual impressions are of four kinds: (1.) Those resulting from the present action of objects upon the nervous system; (2.) Those resulting from the past action of objects, by means of an influence superinduced upon that system; (3.) Those of things which have mutual relations, and admit of comparison; (4.) Those which arise from our wants, and impel us to satisfy them. When our sensibility receives impressions of the first class, it simply *feels;* of the second, it recalls feeling, or *remembers;* of the third, it feels relations, or *judges;* of the fourth, it feels desire, or *wills.** These propositions are worked out in clear and vigorous language, and with a clinching logic to which nothing can be denied, *if* the premises be granted.

The *Projet d'Elémens d'Idéologie* was well received, especially in those Central Schools of the Republic to which the author had expressly addressed himself. Several professors made it a text-book for their lectures. But ideology was soon banished, by authority, from the curriculum of the Central Schools, to its author's great dissatisfaction. The second part of the *Elémens,* containing an elaborate and valuable treatise on grammar, appeared in 1803. The third part—a treatise on logic—followed two years later. Ten more years elapsed before the publication of the fourth

* *Elémens d'Idéologie,* i, 39—74, *seq.*

and of a part of the fifth divisions of the work, which were published together in 1815. The bulk of this latter volume is, in substance, a treatise on social economy. Had the author's plan been carried out, the *Elémens d'Idéologie* would have comprised three main divisions, each consisting severally of three parts. Thus, (1.) The introduction of Ideology; (2.) the *Grammar;* and, (3.) The *Logic,* together, formed (I) a "History of our means of knowing." In like manner, treatises on (4.) *Social Economy;* (5.) *Morals;* (6.) *Government;* formed (II) "The application of our means of knowing to the study of the will and of its results;" and finally, treatises on (7.) *Physics;* (8.) *Geometry;* (9.) *Calculation (calcul);* formed, collectively, (III.) "The application of our means of knowing, to the study of beings extraneous to ourselves" (*l'étude des étres qui ne sont pas nous*).*

Discussion on Ideology in the Academy.

The *Elémens d'Idéologie* became the occasion of a remarkable discussion in the French Academy. De Tracy entered it, in 1808, as the successor of his old friend Cabanis. He made the eulogy of Cabanis an elaborate glorification of this "sensational" philosophy,—according to which the house is identical with the tenant. "All our ideas come from the senses." "To think is to feel." "In the nerves, we have the man." By the Director of the day, Count de Ségur, these doctrines were differently regarded. He reminded De Tracy of his own saying that "Every *system* of metaphysics is a romance." Surely, it could not be his intention to erect into a "system"—certainly as much a romance as the rest, but stripped of their attractions—doctrines, of which the smallest mischief would be to destroy all charm in the present, and all hope of the future; to reduce glory into organic combinations, and to resolve noble passions into coarse sensations; thus "lower-

* *Elémens d'Idéologie,* iii, 520—521.

ing human existence; disenchanting earth; and depopulating heaven." Tracy's speech had its full share of complimentary phrases for "the hero who is the admiration of the universe." He who had danced with Marie Antoinette,* and had fought by the side of La Fayette, did not foresee that he had yet before him the task of moving, in the French Senate, the dethronement of Napoleon.

The sha-
dows of old
age.

Like so many other vast designs, both in Philosophy and Literature, and like so many of which the interruption has entailed a much greater loss on the world—it was the fate of the *Elémens d'Idéologie* to be scarcely half completed. "Nothing more of all this is now permitted to me. This fragment is my last writing,"† are the touching words with which he breaks off.‡ The gradual coming on of blindness, which after a time became total, to be followed by an only partial restoration of sight, would probably not, of itself, have sufficed to daunt the perseverance of so resolute a man. Indeed, he so underwent a very painful operation, as to show that the fortitude which had been evinced so signally in the Carmelite Prison, was still intact. But the mind had lost its elasticity. Its dearest friendships had been broken by death. The days had come when the strongest is forced to say, " I have no pleasure in them."

---

* The famous " Ideologist " had once been known in Parisian circles as " le beau danseur de la reine."

† *Elémens d'Idéologie*, v, 523.

‡ It is stated by the continuators of Quérard (*La Littérature Française Contemporaine*, iii, 521), that Compagnoni's Italian translation, published at Milan in 1819, contains an additional portion of the fifth part, which has not appeared in French. I am unable either to verify a statement so opposed to M. de Tracy's express assertion, or to deny it. But no such additional matter appears in the subsequent translation of a selection of De Tracy's writings in the *Collezione dei Classici Metafisici* (Pavia, 1822—26), now before me.

To this man they brought a special sorrow. The bright era he had hailed as ensuring a "development of reason and an increase of happiness which we vainly seek to estimate by the example of past ages,"* had but dawned, to vanish quickly behind thick clouds :

> "Another race had been, and other palms were won."

How far the chastened spirit, in its latest moments, ever realised to itself the hollowness of that philosophy which conjoined the highest conceptions of the dignity and sacredness of man's rights and capabilities upon earth, with utter insensibility to his power of living a divine life within himself, and of maintaining the faith "that looks through death," we cannot know.

It is certain that the long and deep melancholy that settled around the close of a stirring and brilliant career, never obstructed those acts of habitual beneficence which testified how much the man was better than his teaching. Sensationalism is truly a creed which tends to "disenchant earth and to depopulate heaven." But many a deed of mercy contained the implicit refutation of a doctrine to which the doer still lovingly clung. The man to whom belief was humiliation; who neither knew, nor, according to his own theories, could know, whether or not he had an immortal soul; whether or not there is a God; could yet find it in his heart to build a church for the consolation of humble believers, to whom faith is instinctive and doubt unknown.

Of the minor works of De Tracy, little need be said. The most noticeable of them is the *Commentaire sur l'Esprit des Lois*, first published in Philadelphia in 1811. This treatise had been sent to Jefferson, in the original French, in June, 1809. At that day, it was not at all

De Tracy's Commentaire sur l'Esprit des Lois.

* *Elémens d'Idéologie*, ii, 11.

suited for the meridian of Paris. Jefferson caused it to be translated, and called it "the most precious gift the present age has received." In 1814, the anonymous American book attracted the attention of Dupont de Nemours, who brought it to De Tracy, as a book well worthy to be naturalized in France. At first, De Tracy evaded any expression of his opinion. When Dupont, shortly afterwards, resumed the subject, and spoke of an intention to translate the work, he took the MS. from the drawer, and placed it in his hands. When, at length, the book appeared in French, it passed quickly through several editions, and was thrice translated into Spanish.

The political career of De Tracy closed with the fall of Napoleon. He had always been one of the small knot of temperate but firm opponents of the prevalent policy, who redeemed the Senate from political insignificance. He was now one of the five senators appointed to draw up the project of a "constitutional act." Three others of the five were members of the old circle at Auteuil. Lewis XVIII made De Tracy a Peer of France under the new constitution, but he rarely appeared in the Chamber. The course of events was little in harmony with his convictions or his hopes. To listen to a few favourite authors; to converse occasionally with the sadly lessened group of familiar friends; to keep up the accustomed round of kindly deeds, were now the only employments which diversified the home-life of an affectionate family. As age crept on, his thoughts dwelt more and more apart. He was wont to spend not a little of his time in gazing from a window on the passing clouds—his eyes still sufficed for that. "I suffer, therefore I am," he would sometimes say. To the last he entertained a fond remembrance of his early pilgrim-

Close of De Tracy's political career.

age to Ferney; and Voltaire was always the author he most preferred to have read to him. His sensational "philosophy" had carried him no higher.

The courtier of Marie Antoinette, the fellow-soldier of Lafayette, the senator who moved the dethronement of Napoleon, lived to wander, curiously peering about him, amidst the barricades of July, and to hear of, if not to witness, the many stirring incidents of the first six years of the reign of King Lewis Philip. He died on the 6th March, 1836, at the age of eighty-two. The wish expressed by M. Flourens beside the grave, that his writings, —which are very widely scattered,—should be collected, as his fittest memorial, has not yet been accomplished.

CHAPTER VII.

CHEATEAUBRIAND AND NAPOLEON I.—THE WRITER, THE
EXILE, THE STATESMAN, AND THE ACADEMICIAN.—AN
IMPERIAL AUDIENCE AT SAINT CLOUD.—THE PUBLIC
LIFE OF CHATEAUBRIAND UNDER THE RESTORATION.—
THE *MEMOIRS FROM BEYOND THE GRAVE.*

THREE years later than Destutt de Tracy, Chateaubriand
entered the Second Class of the Institute. His fame had
begun with the *Génie du Christianisme*, a vigorous and
timely protest, in substance, against some of the doctrines
of which De Tracy was the apostle. But when one reads
the racy, expansive, and most characteristic *Mémoires
d'outre tombe*, one regrets to think—notwithstanding the
solemn words which stand on their title page—"*Sicut
nubes; quasi naves; velut umbra,*"—that what Chateaubriand
chiefly saw in Christianity was its respectability, its political
usefulness, and its poetry.

His old age, like that of De Tracy, was often oversha-
dowed by deep gloom. Standing once on the banks of the
Lido, he was heard to say :—" The wind that blows on a
hoary head never blows from a happy shore."

His life, in its vicissitudes and in its thickly crowded
memories, is one of the most marvellous among the many
remarkable lives which have been led by Frenchmen who
had attained manhood before the breaking out of the Revolution of 1789, and who survived to witness the Revolution

of 1848. Born and bred in a province of France, in which the noble was still honoured, and the priest still revered, Chateaubriand witnessed, in the castles of Brittany, a mode of life, almost feudal in its family relations and its social dependencies. Shorn, indeed, of some of its ancient glories, but still invested with the charms of a sombre magnificence, elsewhere at that date unequalled, the old " regime " yet lived in the ancestral chateau of Combourg, of the daily routine of which Chateaubriand has drawn a memorable picture, with a master's hand.

He had had, too, some glimpses of the traditional splendours of the Versailles of Lewis XIV as they were handed down to the courtiers of Marie Antoinette. When Chateaubriand first saw that fascinating woman he was struck, he says, with a peculiarity in her smile, which he had never observed in any other woman. The remembrance of that smile enabled him to identify her remains, when the corpse of the poor queen was exhumed from its obscure resting place, under his official superintendence, in 1815.

During the last struggles of the Monarchy, he was exploring the lakes and the forests of the New World. It was in the hut of an American backwoodsman, near the Blue Mountains, that the news reached him of the flight of Lewis XVI to Varennes. He had conversed with Washington at Mount Vernon about the war of American Independence, about the taking of the Bastille, and about the discovery of a North-west passage; and he had conversed with Napoleon about Egypt, about the traditions of the Arabs, and about the evidences of Christianity. He had lived in a country town of England as a French teacher, and as a writer or translator of pamphlets, for daily bread; and he had lived in London as the Ambassador of Lewis XVIII. He had refused an Embassy

offered by Napoleon, in order that he might testify unmistakeably his abhorrence of the execution of the Duke of
Enghien. He had resigned an Embassy accepted from
Charles X, that he might emphatically condemn the insane
" Ordinances of July."   His latest hours were saddened
by the rumbling of that terrible cannonade which, in June,
1848, trampled down the destructive plots of Communism
in blood.   But he lived long enough to hear that civilization had triumphed, although at fearful cost, and he died
with the conviction that there was no need to despair of
the Future of France.

François René de Chateaubriand was the youngest of
ten children, and was born at Saint Malo on the 4th of
September, 1768. His childhood was passed at Combourg,
which he thrice revisited. On the last occasion, when on
his way to America, he found it a ruin. He had only
courage to glance, through the trees, at the deserted ter-
race, which he never trod again. The old donjon tower
still rears its turrets from its rocky base, but the fine oak-
woods, which once sheltered it, have quite disappeared.

In Brittany, Chateaubriand received holy orders, at the
hands of the Bishop of St. Malo, as a mere preliminary to
his entrance into the knightly Order of Malta. He moralizes
this strange desecration by the thought that, after all, the
revenues of some benefice or other would have been better
spent in maintaining a soldier and his sword, than in
enabling some dissolute Abbé to flaunt his mantilla in the
drawing-rooms and boudoirs of Paris. When he himself
reached the Capital, the first sight that met his eyes was an
insurrection.

When he returned to France, after his long travels in
America, he had scarcely rested his foot before he joined

the Emigration, and served in the "Army of the Princes." Left for dead, in a ditch before Thionville, he recovered, and fled to England. Here he set himself to such fitful and repugnant penwork as the journalist Peltier, and others of the same stamp, found for him, and his remuneration was such as very nearly led—according to his own statement in the preface (as originally printed) to *Atala*—to literal starvation. A chamber companion of his, in those days— they lived on the attic floor of one of those wretched-looking houses which abut on a large burial ground in Marylebone—did actually die at his side, he says, for lack of food.

Thus struggling with fortune, and gaining a livelihood, now by translating obscure pamphlets, and now by teaching French to such pupils as he could obtain, Chateaubriand began to nourish a literary ambition, which, in a very few years, was to be signally gratified. His first work, the *Essai sur les Révolutions*, was the occasional occupation of two years, and was published in London, in 1796. Its main drift is to draw parallels, both of events and of persons, between the French revolution and former revolutions, ancient and modern, in various countries. It partakes strongly of that pseudo-philosophic and sceptical tone, which is the special characteristic of the eighteenth century, and also of the bitter impatience of misfortune, always so natural to the eager appetencies of youth. This essay, as published, was intended to be but the prologue of a larger work. But the task was never resumed. The author outgrew both his incredulity and his misanthropy, and the interval of a very few months saw him busily employed on the *Génie du Christianisme*, as a sort of expiation for the *Essai sur les Révolutions*. How this great change was wrought in his mind he has himself narrated :—" My mother, having been thrown into a dungeon at seventy-two years of age, expired amidst wretchedness, and her last moments were embittered by the remembrance of my wanderings from the right path; whilst dying, she conjured one of my sisters to bring me back to the religion in which I had been nurtured. When my sister's letter reached me in my exile, she also was no more. She, too, had died of the consequences of her imprisonment during the Reign of Terror. These two voices issuing from the grave—one death acting as interpreter to another—touched me to the heart; I became a Christian. . . . . I wept, and I believed."

The printing of the *Genius of Christianity* had been commenced in London in 1799; but the work was not published until April, 1802, nearly two years after Chateaubriand's return to France. The brilliant success of *Atala* —an episode of the *Genius of Christianity*, and the fruit of the author's meditations amongst the American forests— paved the way for that poetical *Retrospect of the services which Christianity has rendered to man and to society*, which unquestionably was of no mean influence in checking the more outrageous blasphemies, and the grosser forms of irreligion, that had so run riot during the worst days of the Revolution. It must suffice to say of this book, that I adopt, concerning it, the words of its first critic, Fontanes, in an article which was published within a very few days of the work's appearance :—

"The author," says the future Grand Master of the University of France, "has aimed at presenting, not the theological proofs of religion, but the picture of its benefits; he appeals rather to the feelings than to the reason. . . . . He depicts religion as occupied in placing sentinels, as it were, on all the paths of misfortune to discover and to

succour it. . . . . Piety founds hospitals, endows colleges,
provides education, protects the arts in monasteries, pre-
serves and interprets the manuscripts in which is deposited
all the genius of the ancients, and without which we should
be poor indeed ; it traverses Europe, distributing benefits,
reclaiming waste lands, multiplying harvests, peopling
desert countries.   But there is a grander spectacle still
than this !   From the obscurity of their cells intrepid men
fly to holy conquests.   They encounter every danger, and
reach the very extremities of the earth, to save souls,—to
civilize humanity."*

Chénier, Ginguené, and others of the same school,
attacked the book with much violence ; but its success was
immense, and was testified—little to the author's satisfaction—by its surreptitious reprint in two distinct piratical
editions, both, I believe, printed at Avignon.   Chateaubriand gives an amusing account of his chase of the pirate.
No sooner had he alighted in Avignon than a hawker
offered him some books for sale, amongst which he found
Atala, in three several editions, all of them counterfeit.
By going from one bookseller to another, he at last ferreted
out the publisher, to whom he was of course personally
unknown, and purchased of him the four volumes of the
Genius of Christianity, for the sum of nine francs.   The
worthy bookseller, who was living in a handsome house,
with courtyard and garden, bestowed liberal praises, both
on the work and on its author.   "I thought," adds the
latter, "I had found the magpie on its nest ; but before
twenty-four hours were over, weary of following in the
track of fortune, I made a compromise with the robber for
a mere trifle."   Independently of these unauthorized
reprints, five considerable editions were sold within three

* *Moniteur Universelle*, 28 Germinal, An X. (April 18, 1802.)

years, and the work was translated into English,* German,
Dutch, Spanish, Italian, and Russian.

The *Genius of Christianity* had been dedicated to Napoleon, who at that time appeared to Chateaubriand to be
"one of those men whom Providence, when weary of
punishing the crimes of a people, sends to it, in token of
reconciliation." This dedication, and the interest excited
by the book, led to an interview between the First Consul
and the future author of the pamphlet, *De Buonaparte et
des Bourbons*.

"After the adoption of the Concordat by the Legislative
Body in 1802, Lucien, then Minister of the Interior, gave an
entertainment to his brother. I was invited, ... and
was in the gallery when Napoleon entered; he made a
favourable impression on me. I had never before seen
him, except at a distance. His smile was pleasing and
attractive; his eye most striking, especially from the manner in which it was set beneath his eyebrows, and his calm,
thoughtful forehead. He had not yet acquired anything
charlatanical in his glance; there was nothing theatrical or

---

* It may deserve to be mentioned, that this English translation,—the
title of which runs, *The Beauties of Christianity*, by F. A. de Chateaubriand. *Translated from the French* by F. Shoberl; *with a Preface and Notes*
by the Rev. H. Kett,—is disfigured by a dishonest practice, which is but
too common, under more or less disguise, and which cannot be too much
reprobated. With singular temerity, it is avowed, in the preface—as
though the fact were a recommendation—that, "to render the work
more agreeable to the Protestant reader, a few chapters and paragraphs,
relative to the tenets of the Church of Rome, are omitted, and a few
paragraphs are softened."—(Preface, pp. xvii, xviii.) In the same preface, a criticism on the work, by Watson, Bishop of Llandaff, is thus
quoted:—"This work is not calculated for the instruction of philosophers, but it will enlarge the views of the ignorant, it will arrest the
attention of the thoughtless, and it will give an impulse to the piety of
sober-minded men. There are passages in it which emulate the eloquence of Bossuet."

affected in his manner. A prodigious imagination animated this cold politician; he never could have been what he was, had not the Muse been there; Reason accomplished that which the poet's thought conceived. Every man who performs great things in the course of his life, must always be compounded of two natures; for he must be capable both of inspiration and of action; the one conceives, the other accomplishes.

Chateaubriand's first interview with Napoleon.

" Napoleon perceived and recognised me : by what outward sign he can have guessed who I was, I cannot imagine. When he advanced towards me, none knew of whom he was in search, and the ranks opened on every side to receive him; every one seemed to hope that the Consul would stop before him. He appeared to feel a certain degree of impatience at these mistakes. I drew back behind my neighbours. Napoleon suddenly raised his voice, and, addressing me, said, 'Monsieur de Chateaubriand!'

" I remained standing alone before him, for the crowd had retired and quickly re-formed in a circle, around the interlocutors. Napoleon accosted me with perfect simplicity, without paying me any compliments, without wasting time on indifferent questions; without preamble he spoke to me at once of Egypt and of the Arabs, as if I had been on terms of intimacy with him, and as if we were only continuing a conversation which had been already commenced between us.

" ' I have been always struck,' he said, ' when I saw the Sheikhs falling on their knees in the midst of the desert, turning towards the east, and touching the sand with their foreheads; what was this unknown thing which they adore towards the east?'

" Napoleon then interrupted himself, and, without any transition, passed abruptly to another idea. 'Christianity!

5

the ideologists have wanted to make it a mere astronomical system; but even should they succeed, do they think to persuade me that Christianity is a small thing? If Christianity is only an allegory of the movement of the spheres, the geometry of the stars, the *esprits forts* may do their utmost, but, in spite of themselves, they cannot help yet leaving sufficient greatness to the "*infâme*." '

"Napoleon quickly left me. Like Job, 'I felt as though, in the night, a spirit had passed before me; the hair of my flesh stood up. It stood still, but I could not discern the form thereof: an image was before mine eyes, and I heard a voice.' My days have been a succession of visions: heaven and hell have been continually opened above my head and beneath my feet, but I have never had time to fathom either their darkness or their light. A single time, on the shores of the two worlds, I met the man of the past age and the man of the present—Washington and Napoleon. I conversed a moment with both; both sent me back into my solitude; the first with a benevolent and kindly wish, the second by a crime.

"I remarked, that as Napoleon walked about amongst the crowd, he cast upon me a much more scrutinizing glance than he had done when he was speaking to me. I also followed him with my eyes—

> ' Chi è quel grande, che non par che curi
> L'incendio ? ' "

Immediately after this interview, Napoleon determined to send Chateaubriand to Rome, as Secretary of Legation to Cardinal Fesch, then Ambassador to the Holy See. It was during this residence in the Eternal City that Chateaubriand conceived the plan—and perhaps began the execution—of the work which is usually regarded as his masterpiece, *Les Martyrs*. But not even literature was suffered to interfere with the duties of his office, which he so discharged as to win the then coveted approbation of him, who already, in the eyes of the multitude, was "the foremost man of all the earth."

Two years afterwards, having returned from the Roman embassy, Chateaubriand was named Minister Plenipotentiary in the Valais. But it was on the eve of that sinister day, on which the last of the Condés was shot in the ditch of Vincennes, "within," to use Chateaubriand's own words, "four paces of the oak beneath which Saint Lewis had dispensed justice." On the evening of that day, whilst all mouths were sealed with fear and stupor, Chateaubriand sent in his resignation. Napoleon has himself recorded the deep impression produced upon him by this manly and noble protest. In recounting the circumstances in his Memoirs, Chateaubriand has very naturally entered into a somewhat elaborate discussion on the much-vexed question —Who are the persons on whom the chief guilt of this murder should rest? His long examination results in the conclusion that Talleyrand was the main culprit; but that Napoleon himself cannot be acquitted of personal responsibility for the crime. Talleyrand, he says, suggested, and Napoleon adopted it. Chateaubriand did not—like some others—wait for the lion's decrepitude, before he became the lion's assailant. His condemnation of the crime was most loudly uttered when its authors were still in the high places of power.

Chateaubriand's emotion at the death of Enghien, and his resignation of his embassy.

After his withdrawal from the diplomatic service of the Empire, Chateaubriand lived a very retired life, partly in Paris, and partly in the south of France, diversified, however, by a brief tour in Switzerland. In 1806, he carried into execution a long-cherished project of Eastern travel.

Having visited Greece, Constantinople, Syria, and the Holy Land—a tour so charmingly described in the *Itinéraire de Paris à Jerusalem*—he returned to Egypt, the old Punic land, and Spain.   He may be said to have been one of the last persons who visited the Turkish Empire, whilst it still retained all its ancient forms and customs, and something of its ancient vigour.   The revolutions he had seemed to leave behind him soon extended even to Greece, to Syria, and to Egypt.

His return to his country was soon embittered by a painful bereavement, under circumstances very similar to those which marked the death of the Duke of Enghien, devoid, however, of the guilt which must always attach to that event.   Armand de Chateaubriand, who was shot on the plain of Grenelle, in March, 1809, had been taken in flagrant conspiracy against the established government of France.   After incessant but fruitless efforts to save his cousin's life, our author wished, on the day of execution, to accompany his old comrade in the " Army of the Princes," to his last battle-field.   He could find no carriage, and had to run on foot to the mournful scene, where he arrived a moment too late ;—Armand had been already shot against the wall of Paris.   " When I walk," he says—writing in 1839 — "on the Boulevard of the plain of Grenelle, I pause to look at the mark of the bullet still visible on the wall."

The execution of Armand de Chateaubriand.

Chateaubriand's election into the Academy, as the successor of Chénier, occurred in the spring of 1811.   He was reluctant, he says, to offer himself, being convinced that his election would involve him in new conflict with the imperial government.   When Mme. de Vintimille took the candidate to pay his visit to Morellet, the

Chateaubriand's visit to Morellet.

"Father of the Academy," they found the old Abbé asleep in his library, beside a copy of the *Itinéraire de Paris à Jerusalem*, which had dropped from his hands. Suddenly awakened by the announcement of his visitor, he started up with the exclamation, "There are some long-spun passages" (*Il y a des longueurs*). I told him, says the author, that I saw it plainly, and would abridge them in a new edition. "He promised me his vote, notwithstanding *Atala*." Morellet had criticised *Atala*, as well as the *Itinéraire*, and with more severity.

Chateaubriand's election had been carried after opposition, but by a large majority, including men of very different opinions. When his intended address came before the official persons, his supporters were in consternation. The discourse is a notable example both of the author's strength and of his weakness. Admirable for its defence of free thought, in a strain which the consciousness of personal peril raised at times from rhetoric into true eloquence, it is marvellous for its Cimmerian darkness on a topic which was yet perpetually in Chateaubriand's mouth. He wields prose like a poet when he asserts the impossibility of isolating literature from the social interests of men, without emasculating it. When he comes to enforce the correlative truth that writers, individually, ought rather to feel proud of obscurity, than to seek personal fame—as some had done—by betraying their country, he sinks into platitudes, and then points his argument by adducing as an example, the conduct, at " a time of public calamity," of JOHN MILTON.

His proposed Discourse at reception in the Academy.

An English reader of this generation, may well pause, in momentary amazement, to think if colourable occasion for such a fancy could, by chance, have arisen from any mistaken incident of the life of the poet, who, at a time of unquestionable public calamity, sat in that humble tenement in Artillery Walk—

Chateaubriand on Milton.

"Darkness before, and danger's voice behind,"*

intent on the composition of *Paradise Lost*. But, if he reads on, for another sentence or two, he finds that the "time of public calamity" was not the time of Charles II—when the Portsmouths and the Buckinghams were in their glory, and the Clarendons in exile—but the time of Vane, Blake, and Cromwell; and that Milton, as some atonement "for the miseries he had brought upon his country," assigned to the powers infernal, depicted in his great poem, "the torments, the passions, and the remorse, of the men of whose fury he had himself partaken."

It was not destined that a Parisian audience should listen to this luminous utterance on English literature. After much discussion, and many conflicting opinions, the historian Daru, a member of the Academy, carried the MS.

A scene at Saint Cloud —Napoleon I as a literary critic.

to Napoleon, who not only read it, but revised it. All that was said of the folly of the attempt to sever literature from affairs; all that was said of Milton; and many of the remarks on Chénier, he struck out. He then summoned Daru to his presence. Passing through an antichamber, in which many dignitaries of the Empire were assembled, the Academician found the Emperor with Chateaubriand's MS. in his hand. What followed was a monologue, uttered, as Daru tells us, partly in a quiet and partly in a resounding voice :—"Had this speech been delivered in its original form," said Napoleon, "I would have shut up the

* "Yet not alone, nor helpless to repel
   Sad thoughts; for, from above the starry sphere,
   Come secrets, whispered nightly to his ear;
   And the pure spirit of celestial light
   Shines through his soul,—that he may see and tell
   Of things invisible to mortal sight."

Institute. I cannot tolerate this sort of thing. I will suffer neither these indiscreet reminiscences, nor these reproaches of the past, nor this tacit censure of the present, although mixed with praise. If the author were here, before me, I would say to him : You, sir, are not of this country. Your admiration and your desires are elsewhere. You comprehend neither my acts nor my intentions. Well, if you are ill at ease in France, leave it. We do not understand one another, and it is I who am master here. You do not appreciate my work, and, were I to permit you, you would spoil it. Depart, sir, cross the frontier. Leave France in peace and unity, under the Government which it needs." The more emphatic words of this outburst were heard in the antichamber. When Daru again passed through, he was, to his amazement, received with icy coldness. His greetings met averted eyes. His questions brought scarcely audible replies. The courtiers were under the impression that it was he, himself, who had just undergone sentence of transportation.

Chateaubriand's Discourse, with its imperial corrections, was, of course, never delivered. But it was printed, by imperial authority, *for circulation in the country*. There was a threat that, unless he composed another address, his election would be annulled. But ultimately, and chiefly, as it seems, by the influence of Mme. Regnauld (de Saint Jean d'Angély), the reception took place, without any formal oration at all. "The women of that day," says Chateaubriand, very characteristically, "interposed their beauty between power and evil fortune."

The remaining years of the Empire were chiefly spent by Chateaubriand in literary employments ; with the close of the Empire his literary career may be said to have terminated, and his active career as a statesman to have begun.

His writings under the Restoration were almost exclusively political. They commenced with the famous tract—*De Buonaparte et des Bourbons.*

This political manifesto is now deservedly forgotten. It was remarkable for ability, but still more remarkable for bitter party spirit. An eminent critic, by no means unfavourably disposed towards Chateaubriand, has characterised it as the "most virulent libel that was ever written." But this is the less surprising, inasmuch as, although it was composed within hearing of the cannonade of the Allies, it was none the less at the peril of the author's life; for even then, at times, the chances of war seemed to favour Napoleon.

Chateau-briand in office.
Of Chateaubriand's career as the Diplomatist and the Minister of the Restoration, it is not necessary to say much. His personal sympathies, and his intense hatred of the system of the Empire, led him at times into the ranks of the most bigoted and outrageous of "the supporters of the throne and the altar." But to two grand principles he was always faithful. The liberty of the press, and the integrity of representative government, ever found in him a faithful and watchful defender. With reference to these principles, at least, he might honestly assert that "the goals of his political life had always been the same."

On the accession to power of the administration of M. de Villèle, Chateaubriand was sent as ambassador, first to Berlin and afterwards to London. In September, 1822, he crossed the Alps to represent France at the Congress of Verona. At this council of kings he pleaded, with very small success, the cause of the Greeks, and defended, with better fortune, what he deemed to be French interests in the complicated affairs of Spain.

The Spanish war.
It has been said that it was the Congress of Verona which forced the Spanish war upon M. de Villèle, and

M. de Villèle who thrust it upon Chateaubriand, when he succeeded M. de Montmorency as minister of foreign affairs. Chateaubriand's own account of the matter, however, in his *History of the Veronese Congress*, is very different; he there avows that he advocated the war, and influenced the decision of the Congress. And it is thus that he defends the course that he adopted :—"Let people imagine to themselves Ferdinand reigning, reasonably, at Madrid, under the rod of France [*sous la verge de la France*], our southern frontier in safety, Iberia no longer able to let England and Austria loose upon us; let them figure to themselves *two or three Bourbon monarchies in America*, forming, for our advantage, a counterpoise to the commercial influence of the United States and of Great Britain; let them imagine our cabinet powerful enough to insist upon a modification of the treaties of Vienna; our ancient frontier recovered, thrust back, extended into the Low Countries, into our old Germanic departments; and then let them say whether for such results the Spanish war was not rightly undertaken."*

It were idle to refute so silly a piece of rhodomontade. The Spanish war was both needless and unjust. It had neither a legitimate beginning nor an avowable object. Yet this weak and foolish defence of it came from a man who, in other days, had fought gallantly and suffered magnanimously on the side of constitutional liberty against triumphant despotism,—and from a Minister who while there was yet time to pause upon the brink, had been distinctly warned by a wiser Statesman than himself of the inevitable results.†

* *Congrès de Vérone*, (1838,) tom. ii, p. 338.
† See the Despatches of Canning to Chateaubriand, Jan. 21 and 27, 1823. *Congrès de Vérone*, tom. i, pp. 330—349.

But the manly counsels of Canning were offered in vain ; and the invasion of Spain by the contemptible Duke of Angoulême remains an indelible stain on the political life of Chateaubriand.

Chateau-
briand in op-
position. Despite this momentary and unfortunate union with the ultra-royalist faction, Chateaubriand was soon compelled to resume his natural attitude of antagonism to it. And he fought with his usual vigour. In the *Journal des Débats*, and elsewhere, nearly all the remaining measures of the administration of Villèle were riddled by his heavy cannonade. The reduction of the dividends—the censorship of the press—the sacrilege bill—the dissolution of the National Guard—were all under fire in their turn. At length the Villèle Ministry was forced to surrender.

Under that of M. de Martignac, which succeeded, M. de Chateaubriand accepted the embassy to Rome, and took an active part in *managing* the conclave which placed Cardinal Annibale della Genga (Leo XII) as the successor of Pius VII on the pontifical throne. He strenuously opposed the measures which marked the fatal entrance into power of the Polignac faction, and on learning its determination to issue the famous "Ordinances," he gave in his resignation. During the three days of July, he was at Dieppe. Immediately on being apprised of the real character of the events which were taking place, he hastened to Paris. When he crossed the barricades on his way to the Chamber of Peers, he was recognised by the populace ; and the men who had just expelled the elder Bourbons, bore aloft in triumph their tried and faithful servant, just as he was about to make a final and fruitless effort for the race which had rewarded his zealous attachment with disgrace and contumely.

It has been pithily said, that from 1814 to 1825,

Chateaubriand fought for the past against the future; that from 1825 to 1830, he enlisted under the flag of the future against the past; and that after 1830, he laboured to solder, after his fashion, the past and the future together; to graft, as it were, a democratic shoot upon a Bourbon stock; "to fuse together Jacques Bonhomme and Henry V." What is likely to come of such attempts at fusion is now an old tale.

The composition of the *Mémoires d'outre tombe*, was begun in the retirement of a little country-house, near the village of Aulnay, in 1811, and continued at Dieppe in the following year, M. de Chateaubriand having been peremptorily ordered to quit Paris by the Prefect of Police, early in the autumn of 1812. The author's political employments prevented their resumption—save in a fragment or two—until the period of his embassy to Berlin in 1821. In that city, and in London (whither, as we have seen, he also went as ambassador), in 1822, a considerable portion of the book was written. From 1822, when it had reached about one third of its present extent, until 1837, it appears to have been entirely suspended. The remainder of the work was written in 1837 and subsequent years—with the exception, perhaps, of the long and remarkable episode respecting Napoleon, the composition of which bears no date. *Composition of the Memoirs from beyond the Grave.*

M. de St. Beuve (in his *Critiques et Portraits Littéraires*) has given a lively description of the interest excited amongst the brilliant auditories assembled at the Abbaye-aux-bois, in 1834, by the readings of the *Mémoires d'outre tombe*, in their earlier portions, as they were composed. The later volumes were read to a very different audience from that of the Abbaye-aux-bois, and under altered circumstances. Those final readings occurred but a short while before the *The reading of the Posthumous Memoirs.*

Revolution of February. That startling thunder-clap sur-
prised the remaining hearers of the "old man, eloquent,"
into quite other pursuits than literary recitations. Their
numbers had been already diminished by death. And the
eventful career of the writer himself closed in the same
memorable year.

Perhaps, had Chateaubriand written less; had he acted,
occasionally, on the Horatian precept, his works would be
likely to enjoy a longer existence than seems now before
them. But it may, certainly, be said of him, in the
words of a fellow-academician of the next generation, although in a different sense from that in which those words
were written :—"The man's life will" (for some time to
come, at least) "get his books a reading," notwithstanding
their frequent puffy hyperboles and flimsy sentimentalities.

CHAPTER VIII.

NAPOLEON AND THE POETS.—THE ACADEMICIANS DUCIS
AND LEMERCIER,—THE POETRY-PRIZE OF THE BELLE
POULE EXPEDITION.—THE ACADEMY UNDER THE RESTO-
RATION.—THE "LAW OF JUSTICE AND LOVE."

THE relations between the Emperor and the Second Class
of the Institute were never cordial. The "Ideologists" were
his persistent though not always his open opponents. The
poets stood almost equally aloof. Both Ducis and Lemercier had been captivated, for awhile, by the glory of the
Consulate. Ducis, like Chateaubriand, had been alienated   *Ducis' re-
by the murder of the Duke of Enghien. " He has deceived   *vulsion of*
                                                            feeling to-
me, I thought him a Cincinnatus, but he is despotism incar- *wards Napo-*
                                                            leon.
nate." Such was the feeling to which is owing the pun-
gent although one-sided apologue, *Une promenade au Bois
de Satori.* Delille, who had refused to write a " Hymn to
the Supreme Being," at the menacing request of Robespierre, resisted the splendid and reiterated overtures of
Napoleon. Lemercier, who from 1795 to the eve of the
Empire, had been on the most intimate terms with
Napoleon, and who to the end of his long life was wont to   *Lemercier's*
talk of " *Mon ami, le Premier Consul,*" once, with difficulty, *early friend-*
                                                            ship and sub-
brought himself to write some verses on the marriage with   *sequent ani-*
                                                            mosity to-
Maria Louisa. At that date, his nomination to the Aca-   *wards Napo-*
                                                            leon.
demy had just occurred. Shortly afterwards, the imperial
censorship suppressed his tragedy of *Camillus,* in which

the military capacity and courage of the hero is very markedly united with an absolute submission to the laws. Within a few days of that suppression, the Institute had to wait upon the Emperor, on some state occasion. As soon as Napoleon saw Lemercier, he put to him the question,—"Well, M. Lemercier, when will you give us a *good* tragedy?" The poet looked intently at the man whose fortunes were then at their height,—unshaken, as yet, by the campaign of 1812,—and replied, "Soon. *I am waiting.*" Eight years earlier, he had said to the First Consul, "You are amusing yourself with making the bed of the Bourbons. I foretell you that you will not lie in it ten years." The conviction seems to have remained with him amidst the quick-succeeding marvels which had dazzled almost all eyes. It is less to his honour that, although he survived the expedition of the *Belle Poule*, he never learnt, during that long interval, to discriminate between the great and the petty elements of Napoleon's character. He saw quickly enough what was mean, despicable, and transient. He never perceived what was grand and enduring. Only two days before his own death he dragged himself to the Louvre, that he might give a vote against the choice, for the poetry-theme of the year, of "*The return to France of the Ashes of Napoleon.*" Lemercier had sat in the Gallery of the Convention, day after day, amidst the knitting-women, "to see the laws outlawed," until the sights that he had there looked upon wrought on his very features an expression almost of idiocy.* But it seems never to have occurred to him that the man who had, at least, dethroned anarchy, had done a service to

The Poetry-Prize on the return to France of the body of Napoleon.

---

* This curious circumstance has been recorded by a contemporary. So striking was the reflection on his features of the horror in his mind, that some of the regular attendants in that gallery thought him really an idiot, with a mania for speeches.

France, which no subsequent misdoings can justly oblite-
rate from memory.

Lemercier lived long enough to observe that revulsion of
feeling towards Napoleon's memory—amongst men of the
poet's own class—in which he could not share. He also
lived long enough to survive his own works. Great as had
been their influence upon his immediate contemporaries,
they lacked that savour of style which is the condition, not
only of immortality, but even of the continued esteem of a
single generation. His force of character—his resolute
independence of spirit—can never lose their charm. These
were the qualities which made the man greater than the
poet. Lemercier spoke his mind, and spoke it fully, at all
epochs; alike, whether the men at the helm were friends
or foes; whether the views expressed were popular or
unpopular ; and, hence, his fate was pretty much the same
at all epochs. The Committee of Public Safety proscribed
his *Lévite d'Ephraim.* The National Convention suppressed
his *Tartufe Révolutionnaire.* Under Napoleon's censorship he had five several dramas tabooed from the stage.
Under the censorship of Lewis XVIII, his *Démence de
Charles VI* was formally condemned. The reader of the
recently published autobiography—for such it substantially
is—of Victor Hugo, will remember some curious parallel-
isms in the otherwise contrasted careers of the men who
sat in the same Academical chair.

The second reorganization of the Institute, under the
returned Bourbons, restored the old statutes and the old
name of *French Academy*, but struck, for a time, an almost
deadly blow at its honour. The names of " Bonapartist "
and too " liberal " Academicians were indiscriminatingly
struck from the roll by a royal ordinance, to be replaced,

Lemercier's
character
more vigo-
rous than his
works.

Reorganiza-
tion of the
Academy by
Lewis XVIII.

for the most part, by names of abbés, bishops, counts, and
dukes, little known to literature.   By the ultra-royalists,
this was called the " Purification of the Academy."   Very
fitly, the purification was begun by Fouché, and completed
by Vaublanc.   Several of the excluded members were
driven into exile and penury.   Arnault, for example,
was not suffered to rest, even in Belgium, but, at an age
when repose becomes a necessity, was driven from place to
place by the Belgian gendarmerie.   His colleagues honoured
themselves by subscribing, both individually and in the
name of the Academy, towards an edition of his works.
At length, in 1829, he resumed his seat.   Maury, twice
elected, as we have seen, had no successor to commemorate
his singular career.   Etienne lived to re-enter the Academy,
and to fill a conspicuous place in it for many years.   Garat,
too, was, after a time, advised to offer himself as candidate
for a vacant seat.   " My election," he replied, " was
indelible.   Whatever may have been decreed, I am, and I
shall be, of the French Academy as long as I live.   When
I was Home Minister, I gathered up the fragments of the
Academy's Dictionary.   I have since shared in its discussions.   And if I thought that I could now attend without
hindrance, I would go to-morrow, and take my seat with
my colleagues."   Garat must have felt his exclusion the
more keenly, inasmuch as he had always been a little of
the school of that cautious devotee who, we are told, when
he was building a fine church for Divine worship, did not
forget to erect a small chapel for the arch-enemy hard by.
An extreme prudence had not saved him from a bitter
humiliation.

This attempt to compel the Academy into political sub-
serviency had small success.   Some years, indeed, passed
without any open collision between the Government and

the Institute.   But in 1827, M. de Peyronnet, acting under the influence of the Jesuits of Montrouge, anticipated the fatal Ordinances of 1830, by proposing to the Chambers a law which laid new fetters on the press.   The vigorous action of the Academy arrested the project, even after its sanction by a parliamentary majority.   Charles de Lacretelle (although he then held the office of Dramatic Censor) moved the Academy to adopt an energetic protest against a measure which, he said, "cast disgrace on literature, and would be politically disastrous."   The proposal was, with equal warmth, supported by Chateaubriand, by Count de Ségur, by Villemain, and by Lemercier.   It was opposed by La Place and by Cuvier.   The King refused to receive the protest, but it had done its work.   Peyronnet replied to the Academy by an article in the *Moniteur*, in which he used the words " A law of Justice and Love," and thus gave to the abortive Ordinance its famous nickname.   The words were borrowed from *"Les Soirées de St. Petersbourg,"* and no plagiarism was ever less felicitous.   Every Academician who had voted for the protest, and who held any office under the Crown, was immediately dismissed.   Lacretelle lost his office of Examiner of Plays ; Villemain, his Mastership of Requests ; Michaud, his Readership to the King.   The public sympathy with the disgraced Academicians was testified in many ways, and the joy at the defeat of the " Law of Justice and Love," was shown by the illumination of Paris.   This was the overture to the terrible drama of 1830.

Margin note: Noble resistance of the French Academy, and its punishment.

CHAPTER IX.

STRIFE OF CLASSICISTS AND ROMANTICISTS. — THE ACADEMIC CANDIDATURES OF CASIMIR DE LA VIGNE AND OF VICTOR HUGO.

MANY of the receptions during the reign of Lewis Philip present striking illustrations of literary history, and of the varying currents of opinion. I pass over them all, save three.

The early efforts of Casimir de la Vigne.

Like so many other of the men who have conspicuously added to the Academy's fame, Casimir De La Vigne early tried his strength in the annual competitions. He repeatedly obtained the honour of the "Accessit," but it was not his fortune to win a prize. On one occasion the medal was almost in his grasp. But the Academy had said— "*Study creates happiness under all the varied circumstances of human life.*" The young poet turned the assertion into a query—"*Does study create happiness, &c. ?*" The poem was warmly and deservedly applauded, and seemed sure of the prize. An Academical martinet, however, contended that by their rules the liberty taken with the programme was fatal to its claims, and his opinion prevailed. Thenceforth the poet addressed himself to the task of making his way into the Academy by the triumphs of the Theatre. *Les Vépres Siciliennes, Les Comédiens, Le Paria,* were the ovations of two seasons. They were won at the darkest period of the Restoration by works which vibrated with the love of liberty. That "purification" of the Academy which was to prove powerless to arrest its rightful action at a great crisis, was nevertheless sufficient to impede the entrance of obnoxious candidates. When De La Vigne first offered himself, the Academy preferred the Bishop of Hermopolis; when he was again a candidate, the Archbishop of Paris was chosen. Soon, a third vacancy occurred, and his friends were importunate that he should not lose his chance. "No," said he, "if I offered myself a third time, I am sure they would oppose to me the Pope." But then came the splendid success of *L'Ecole des Veillards*, which carried the doors of the Academy by storm. He now obtained twenty-nine votes out of thirty, was opposed by no more prelates, and took his seat on the 7th July, 1825.

His candidature for the Academy.

The inexhaustible controversy between those who would give wings to innovation, and those who would put a drag on it, had at this time its double arena in France. The Classicists and the Romanticists were playing out their lively counterpart of the old strife between Royalists and Liberals. It is not easy, in these days, to form an adequate conception of the violence with which this struggle was at length carried on by a portion of the press. But, when Casimir De La Vigne made his reception speech to the Academy, the contest had as yet scarcely passed the limits of moderation. Deeply imbued with the distinctive merits both of the old school and of the new, he enforced the wisdom of keeping within those limits. He depicted with power and beauty the perplexities of the young dramatic poet encountering, at the outset of his first adventure on that broad ocean which had borne his predecessors to such glorious triumphs, some "Genius of the storm," who terrifies him with stories of the rocks and shoals which await him, and of the shipwrecks they have caused. The Genius

Strife of Classicists and Romanticists.

warns him, above all, to try no new courses; assures him
that beyond the boundary of the now visible horizon, there
is neither star to guide nor tide to bear him on his way;
nothing save disaster and certain ruin. "But," he asked,
"what avail these alarming predictions, if within the poet
there be that which irresistibly urges him to seek new discoveries—to attach his name to some region before unknown?
Danger does but spur him onward. Yet the perils are real.
And the only safe pilot is the poet's conscience, directing
his art, and religiously obeyed. Boldness must be governed
by reason. Contempt of rules is not less absurd than
fanaticism for rules. To thrust a subject into limits which
are plainly repugnant to it, is to immolate Truth to Routine.
To disregard good rules, simply to be singular or to win
momentary applause, is but to evince a new servility more
contemptible than the old." Such counsels are now com-
monplace; they were then much needed. The poet who
gave them contributed powerfully to make them trite.

Within the walls of the Institute the strife for a time
seemed to turn on the admission or the exclusion of Victor
Hugo, the most eminent of the literary revolutionists, and
the founder of their famous "Cénacle."

The *Odes et Ballades* had been published in 1822;
Cromwell, in 1827; *Notre Dame de Paris, Marion Delorme,*
and *Les Feuilles d'Automne,* in 1831. The poet was not
admitted into the Academy until 1841. Lemercier, who
was really the precursor of the Romantic school although
he disowned the relationship, had unremittingly opposed
his admission. Lemercier's death became the occasion of
Hugo's election. The public looked for a lively discourse
on the war between the Romanticists and Classicists; it
had to listen, instead, to a grave essay on the duties of

Victor Hugo's long exclusion from the Academy.

Literature towards Society, with especial reference to
political reforms.

The chair was occupied by a man who had himself made His reception in 1841,
by M. de Sal-
vandy.
literature the stepping-stone to a prominent career in
Politics. M. de Salvandy took elaborate pains to impress
upon his new colleague that Victor Hugo, the poet, must
remain a poet, and stand quite aloof from public affairs.
Nor did he stop there. He gave a turn to his reply, hitherto
without example in the Academy's transactions. The
Abbé de Caumartin had received the Bishop of Noyon with
subdued but cutting satire. Languet de Gergy had
tempered his praises of Marivaux with some candid criticisms. Marmontel had amused the audience assembled
to receive Laharpe, by the witty sallies with which he
put into high relief certain contrasts between the deceased Academician, Colardeau, and Laharpe, his successor. Now, for the first time, the President attempted
an exhaustive refutation of the discourse of the new-comer.
The animus was none the less evident for the failure of the
effort. As a reply must needs contain an admixture of
eulogy, M. de Salvandy praised some of Hugo's earliest lyrics,
and paid to his mature works the compliment of saying
that, now and then, they recalled to the reader's mind something of the beauty of the first-fruits of the poet's youth.

Whatever the audience may have thought of the fitness
or the taste of this novel procedure, it must have had the
merit of keeping off all tendency to drowsiness. Instead
of listening to mutual eulogies, there was the excitement
of a pitched battle of wit and subtlety, heightened, perhaps, by the knowledge that the official receiver had done
his best to keep the received outside the door. But the
example, if ever imitated at all, has been much refined upon
in the repetition.

CHAPTER X.

ALEXIS DE TOCQUEVILLE.—HIS WORK ON NORTH AMERICA.
— HIS RECEPTION AT THE ACADEMY. — HIS OTHER
WRITINGS AND POLITICAL LIFE.

CHARLES Alexis Maurice Clerel de Tocqueville was born at
Verneuil, in the department of the Seine and Oise, on the
29th July, 1805. Descended from an ancient family of Nor-
mandy, he was the third son of the Count of Tocqueville, by
his marriage with Mdle. de Rosambo, one of the granddaugh-
ters of the illustrious Malesherbes. This marriage had
been contracted in 1793, and was quickly followed by that
imprisonment during the Terror, which so many of that
eminent family quitted only for the guillotine; a fate from
which the parents of M. de Tocqueville narrowly escaped
by the event of the 9th Thermidor.

Alexis de Tocqueville was educated at the college of
Metz, at first with a view to the military profession, which
had already been adopted by his two elder brothers. But
before his studies were concluded, this intention was
changed. He prepared himself for the bar, to which he
was called in 1825, and then travelled through Italy, before entering into practice. In 1827, he was appointed
judge-auditor at the tribunal of Versailles. The revolution
of 1830 matured in his mind liberal sympathies and aspirations which had not been concealed in gloomier days;
but the only favour which he sought at the hands of the

new government was a commission to examine, jointly with his friend Gustave de Beaumont, and at their personal expense, the penitentiary system of the United States of America. This task they undertook early in 1831, and performed it, exhaustively, during a long tour throughout the States, which occupied the remainder of that year and much of 1832. They were cordially received, and made many friendships.

In 1833, the results of the inquiry were published in a work entitled, *Du Système Pénitentiare aux Etats-Unis, et de son Application en France ; suivi d'un Appendice sur les Colonies Pénales,* &c. This Report traces the history of the American system, and describes the remarkable measure of success which had attended it. It shows that this success was principally due to the local administration which had both originated and worked out the system. It recommends, therefore, that in France power should be given to the Departments, severally, to erect and govern cellular prisons ; insists on the prime necessity of isolation,—labour, —religious instruction,—fit and responsible warders,—in the management of such prisons ; condemns the system of " surveillance " exercised by the French police over released prisoners ; and condemns still more emphatically the punishment of transportation under all its forms. This last feature in the Report is noticeable for its date. In 1832, little attention had yet been aroused to the mischievous consequences of transportation as practised in our own country—consequences now so generally admitted. Our example, indeed, had just then been urged for French imitation by an author, M. de Blosse, whose work was laureated by the French Academy. The creation of special reformatory prisons for juvenile delinquents is also one of the recommendations of this pregnant Report. Its authors, as is usual in

De Tocqueville's inquiry into the penitentiary system.

The Penitentiary system and that of Transportation before the Academy.

such cases, found it uphill work to carry into operation the reforms they recommended ; but both of them had opportunity to urge their views on the attention of the Chamber of Deputies, and important improvements were gradually effected in the French prisons.

Results of De Tocqueville's mission to America. The immediate results, however, pale their fires before the grand result which came but incidentally from the mission of 1831 ; for to it we owe a masterpiece in political literature. Here, also, the date is an important element towards due appreciation. There had already been plenty of travellers in the then "United States," with much curiosity and ample note-books. But the great majority of them had been engrossed by the pettiest objects. Not a few had profited by an openhanded hospitality to turn into ridicule the manners, and to caricature the failings of their The Political Career of Alexis de Tocqueville. hosts. Very different was the ambition of M. de Tocqueville. He was not a republican, either by conviction or by self-seeking. Himself an accomplished member of the polished aristocracy of France, he was little likely to overlook the absence in America of many courtesies and ornaments, materially conducive to the charms of social life. But he carried with him the memory of Revolutions which had terribly disturbed the elegant repose of people who persist in mistaking shadows for substances. In his childhood he had heard of the prisons of the Terror, from the lips of those whose lives they had blighted, and had witnessed the plaudits which welcomed the veterans who had traversed Europe in triumph. In his youth he had twice seen foreign armies overrunning his native land. At his outset in public life, he beheld a king driven swiftly into exile, and a luxurious capital laid at the mercy of insurgents, many of whom were in want of bread. In America, as he saw it, in 1831-32, he found apparent stability, instead of incessant revolution; peaceful enjoyment of the fruits of industry, instead of habitual panic; an almost universal possession of many of the comforts as well as of the mere necessaries of life, instead of the frequent contrasts between lavish splendour and utter penury; and he thought the causes of such disparities must be worth investigating. He certainly had not travelled over the length and breadth of the United States, in such years as 1831 and 1832, without seeing the social landscape in all its aspects, and under all its phases of atmospheric change. He had witnessed disgraceful scenes of popular violence and folly, which induced a friend to ask him how it was possible that he could write of them with such good humour and kindly forbearance. "Ah!" he replied, "had you, like me, been bred up amidst all the miseries of insecurity, political and personal, you would have learned to view the worst that happens in America with calmness."

At the age of thirty-two, De Tocqueville had already burst into European reputation by his famous treatise. American society and manners; the constitution and the dangers of the Union; had been the themes of a score of books, but De Tocqueville's book was the first which analyzed the mechanism and disclosed the motive-power of the body politic. The production of a mind thoroughly cultivated as well as deeply reflective, it was scarcely more remarkable for its contents than for its tacit suppressions. The author's attention was almost exclusively bent on that working out of great social problems which the then United States had offered to his view. But his forbearance proceeded from no lack of power to describe, incisively, the phenomena which lie on the surface of social life, or to paint with vividness the natural beauties of what to most European readers is still a "New World." What he could do in

The previous career of the Author and the Publicist.

that department may be seen in the pages of the *Revue des deux Mondes*.   In his great work, he debarred himself from these attractive topics, in spite of the temptation which such powers present.   He had pondered both the realities and the semblances which America offers to the seeing eye, under the influence of impressions, gained in France, which were destined to colour his whole life.   The traditions of the great overturn of 1793, and of the conquests and fall of Napoleon, were his youthful memories.   With the Revolution of 1830 he had been in close personal contact. What he saw in the States gave him the conviction that the inevitable transition from old to new, which in his own country was still causing such rendings of society, might possibly be brought about at less cost.   And to teach the lesson he had learnt, or believed himself to have learnt, was, thenceforth, the main object of his labours.

In the Institute he succeeded the Count de Cessac, one of the ablest of Napoleon's administrators, who had lived long enough to receive his old master's remains at the Invalides.   But it was not simply because they succeeded men the prime of whose lives had been passed under the Empire, or because recent events had roused the old echoes, that the thoughts of men who had to speak at the Institute seemed drawn so repeatedly and so irresistibly to the era of Napoleon.   They saw the continued vitality of the seed which Napoleon had sown, and which has since borne such conspicuous fruit.   De Tocqueville thought that Frenchmen under Napoleon were at remoter distance from liberty, than at any preceding period of their history.   The Empire, in his view, owed its splendour "to its accidents." "Napoleon was as great as a man can be, without virtue. He carried through an unexampled enterprise.   He rebuilt the whole social edifice, in order to make it a

De Tocqueville's Discourse of reception.

convenient dwelling-place for despotism." In replying to
this address, Count Molé—the President of the day—was
as vigorous and as trenchant as his adversary. The only
"accident" of the Empire, he said, was the Emperor.
With Napoleon, "despotism" was, not the end, but the
means—and the only means—of forcing the swollen river Count Molé's reply.
back into its bed; of restoring to revolutionized France the
habits of order and obedience; of giving her the time for
needful oblivion; of opening, to all, a new era. And
the end was to make France the greatest country on earth.
"Such was Napoleon, as I saw him. But do not think I am
less truthful than you are. It is not I who will dissimulate
a tittle of the misfortune he drew upon France. He wanted
the knowledge where to set the limits of possibility, and
the conviction that Truth and Justice are the best means of
governing men, simply because they *are* Truth and Justice.
Napoleon was, himself, the child of that eighteenth century
which he arraigned so sternly. He lived only by the intellect. He had faith only in the intellect. He believed
that, in the beginning, the world belonged to the strongest,
and that civilization had handed it over to the cleverest. He
dreaded, above all things, the rule of the majority, as being,
under one form or other, the sole return to violence and bar-
barism which, in our times, is possible." Count Molé Molé's re-miniscence of Lamoignon de Malesherbes.
closed his speech by a touching allusion to the illustrious
grandfather of the new Academician :—"I still see his
venerable face, covered with tears. *That* will tell you when
it was that I saw him. He had just ended his sublime
task, and awaited its recompense—the scaffold. But, sir,
it was not in America, it was not amidst a pure democracy,
that the soul of Malesherbes had built itself up."

The first portion of the treatise *De la Démocratie en*

Amérique was published in Paris in 1835. It reached its
fifth edition in 1838, and its thirteenth edition in 1850;
was quickly translated into English by Mr. Henry Reeve,
into Spanish by Sanchez de Bustamante, and into German
by F. A. Aüder. In 1836, the French Academy awarded
to it the Monthyon prize. In 1839, the second part appeared in two volumes, like the former part. As usual,
the continuation was not received with quite so much favour
as its predecessor. In this instance there is cause, I think,
for the opinion, that its distinctive merits themselves, as well
as its distinctive defects, somewhat lessened its popularity.

Seminal
idea of the
" Democracy
in America." The seminal idea of this famous book is, that the irre-
sistible tendency of American institutions, and of American
thought, towards the utmost possible equalization of human
conditions, is the counterpart of a substantially similar tendency in Europe, but is, in America, so developing itself,
as to exhibit at once the ultimate benefits and the contin-
gent perils which that equalization enfolds. In De Tocqueville's opinion, therefore, to portray America is, in a certain
sense, to prefigure Europe; in substance, that is, by no
means necessarily in form; and with the important qualification, that American experience may possibly so influence
European opinion, as to make attainable the benefits, and
avoidable the perils, of a solution of the great social pro-
blem, which, in the main, he believes to be inevitable.
Equality of political power,—and an approach even to
equality of condition, speaking broadly,—must, he thinks,
be realized in Europe as well as in America. Wise and
moderate advances on the part of those who wield government or sway opinion, will, in his opinion, help to realize it
safely. Unwise and indiscriminating resistance may re-
tard its coming, but must at last embitter its unavoidable
rule.

In Part I, after describing the external configuration of North America, and the starting-point of its colonists, he shows what they brought with them. He singles out that old principle of local self-government, from whence all the existing institutions of the country have grown, and traces its progress and its ramifications. He examines the several institutions of the States, marks the growth of their jurisprudence, and the formation of political opinion. He shows how it has come to pass that, in the most rigorous sense of the words, "the people governs;" that not only are the institutions democratic, but all their developments and modes of working are also democratic; that in America the people virtually elect both the law-maker and the administrator of law, whilst itself is the jury which, if it like the law, punishes those who break the law. He dissects the federal constitution, and reconstructs it from its elements, bringing saliently out these three main facts :—(1) That the majority is everywhere and in everything omnipotent; (2) that the peace, prosperity, and even the very existence of *the Union*, lie immediately in the hands of the Supreme Federal Court, "the true moderator," as he terms it, "of the democracy;" (3) that the higher and ultimate security of political freedom, and all that it involves, lies, on the one hand, in the absence of administrative centralisation; on the other, in the universal diffusion of education, property, and the sense of inherent and inalienable rights, throughout the entire community. There is no winking either at the vices or at the perils of democracy. In speaking of the absolute subjection even of the press to the will of the majority, there is such plain-speaking as this :—"No writer, whatever his renown, can escape from the obligation to burn incense before his countrymen. The majority lives in perpetual self-worship. Disagreeable truths reach the ears of Americans only from the voice of a foreigner, or from the lessons of experience."* Elsewhere he says,—"*I know no country in which there is, usually, less independence of mind, less real freedom of discussion, than in America.*"† These words will seem, to some minds, to involve, implicitly, a prediction of what has happened. It has been said by acute observers, that the want of really free discussion has been not the least influential amongst the many causes of the disastrous civil war. But in marking defects, there is, in De Tocqueville, no clamour, no invective, no disdain; uniformly, the anxiety is to indicate a remedy.

Thus far the author had a solid framework of facts, of institutions, of measurable and computable results. His book is a masterpiece of systematic construction. All its parts unite and converge towards weighty and definite conclusions. In advancing to the second part, the demarcations of the subject become necessarily less distinct. There he has to treat of the influence of democracy on (1) intellectual progress; on (2) public feeling (*sentiments*); on (3) manners; on (4) political society. It is much easier to criticise this arrangement than to suggest a better one; to say, for instance (as is obvious), that "public feeling" is very closely allied both with intellectual progress and with manners. A more serious objection may perhaps lie to the universality of the influences ascribed to the one passion for political and social equality. But an excessive estimation of a great subject is probably the unavoidable condition on which we receive great works. At all events, it is certain that the modifications and minor adjustments of any such subject may easily come afterwards, and that minds of smaller calibre will suffice for the task. To the

* *De la Démocratie*, &c., treizième édition, i, 309.
† Id., i, 307.

discoverer of an untrodden region in the world of thought, we can forgive some exaggeration of its treasures.

The wide survey here taken of American society in all its phases, results, on the whole, in a genial estimate of the present, and in far too hopeful auguries of the future. But in describing the intellectual and social results of democracy as they unfold themselves in America, there is as little suppression of the unfavourable features as there was in the analysis of its political results. Thus, for example, in a chapter of the second part, which treats of the special importance to democratic communities of the remoter aims of human action, there occurs this passage :—" As soon as men cease to place their grand aims at a great distance, they are naturally impelled to seek the immediate realization of their pettiest desires ; as if, desparing to live eternally, they must needs act as though they had but a single day to live." This is a warning, for proof of the pertinency of which we need not look so far afield as to America. Much of the book has a like home applicability. There are keen censures in it, which consist simply in putting facts under the light, but the facts so lighted up are by no means exclusively of American growth. This, I think, is one of the causes why the second part was not, like the first, highly lauded in articles, the entire drift and spirit of which was in antagonism with the book reviewed. Instead of this, a reader may perhaps find in one number of a literary journal loud praise, and in another number of the same journal an assertion that " those who follow De Tocqueville are pantheists in politics, and will soon come to pantheism in religion,"*—a hit, assuredly, very wide of the mark. To me it seems that the deficiencies in the book really most obnoxious to criticism are (1), the absence

The lessons to be derived from " Democracy in America."

* *Quarterly Review*, lxvi, 493.

of any adequate estimate of the political effects of the wide extent of sparsely-peopled territory in America;* and (2), the utterly insufficient view which is given of the influences of Protestantism on the American people ; both of them, it may be noted, points which are likely to be very differently regarded in France and in Britain. That *Democracy in America* is the work of a mind saturated with the past glories of France, alarmed at the perils that visibly obstructed her onward path, and intent, above all things else, on her deliverance, is not its least merit. To make American experience subserve French progress, and to convert American mistakes into French safeguards, was the author's constant aim.

Labours in the Chamber of Deputies.

De Tocqueville's political career—as far as respects home politics—was in thorough harmony with the pervading patriotism and the lofty qualities of the book, the fame of which was already world-wide before that career began. He was elected to the Chamber of Deputies by the Department of La Manche in 1839, and in the course of the same year made a valuable report on slavery in the French colonies, proposing its abolition (which was not effected, however, until after the fall of Lewis Philip), with an indemnity to the colonists, as a matter of public utility, "not as a compensation for the loss of that which no man ever had, or could have, any right to possess,"† a proposition which excited great turmoil amongst the colonists. In February, 1840, and again in April (after the formation of

---

* Yet this point was strongly urged upon the attention of the fellow-travellers (in relation to the specific object of their mission), by a letter from the Attorney-General of Maryland, written in January, 1832.

† *Rapport au nom d'une Commission* .... *relative aux Esclaves des Colonies* (*Procès Verbeaux des Séances de la Chambre des Députés, Session de* 1859). Séance du 23ᵉ Juillet.

the Thiers ministry), he strenuously supported motions for
limiting the number of public functionaries in the Chamber
of Deputies.   Repeatedly during that and subsequent
years, he laboured in the promotion of improvements in the
criminal law, and especially in prison discipline.   In
1847, as chairman of the Committee on Algiers, he made
elaborate reports recommending administrative reform
in that colony, and the extension of local powers in secondary matters; and strongly condemning (1) the prevalent
system of attempting to do everything for the colonists,
instead of training them to do most things for themselves;
and (2), a particular pet project of the government for
military agricultural settlements at the public cost,* which
was, however, carried out, but with results strongly confir-
matory of the opposer's views.   His most memorable
speech was that made on the 27th January, 1848, in
which, in the simplest words, but with the utmost possible
incisiveness, he urged every member of the Chamber to put
to himself the question, "What must be the end of that
electoral corruption and that public scandal which I, individually, know to exist?" and then implored the ministers
to change a policy which, said he, "makes the ground
tremble beneath our feet;" concluding with these prophetic
words—"Is it possible you can be undisturbed by that
sough of revolution which is in the wind (*vent de révolution
qui est dans l'air*), which blows we know not whence or
whither, and know as little, be assured of that, whom it will
whirl away?   Is it at such a moment that you can calmly
witness the degradation of public morality?"†   These words

His antici-
pations of
1848.

* *Rapport au nom de la Commission chargée d'examiner le Projet de
Loi relatif aux crédits extraordinaires demandés pour l'Algérie (Procès ver-
baux, &c., Session de 1847, vi, 305—410).*

† *Discours de M. de Tocqueville, dans la discussion du Projet d'Adresse,*
Séance du 27 Janv., 1848 (*Moniteur*, 28th Jan., 1854).

were timely. They were uttered exactly four weeks before the Revolution of February; but many ears are deaf to the wisest charmer.

Political career under the Republic, and the Empire of Napoleon III.
After that revolution, the Department of La Manche returned M. de Tocqueville to the National Assembly by a majority of 110,711 votes over his next competitor. He was third on a list of fifteen names. He voted for the banishment of the House of Orleans; became vice-president of the Committee of Public Instruction, and a member of the Committee on the Constitution, and took a very noticeable part in the discussions on the "rights of labour." In one of his speeches on this topic, the socialistic theories were, for the first time in the National Assembly, fairly grappled with. He branded "socialism" as an energetic and pertinacious appeal to the lower passions of mankind; as a system of which the basis was a thorough mistrust of liberty, a hearty contempt for man individually; as, in a word, a lust for the old servitude in a new livery. In 1849, after representing France at the Brussels Congress, he became Minister of Foreign Affairs, and in that capacity he strenuously vindicated the policy of the memorable expedition to Rome, to which, in its origin, he had not been a party, and the ultimate direction of which was to fall into quite other hands. The defence, assuredly conscientious, seems to me just as certainly fallacious. Here, however, it can neither be described nor appreciated. But it must be mentioned that one of the chief grounds of that defence in his mouth was, that the expedition tended "to prevent a return of the old abuses. . . . . You must never," he told the Assembly, "lose sight of that which now becomes the main point,—that we desire to secure to the States of the Church really liberal institutions."*

* *Discours de M. de Tocqueville*, &c., 6 Août, 1849 (*Moniteur*, 7th Aug. 1849).

M. de Tocqueville's ministry of foreign affairs lasted only five months.   When (31st Oct., 1849) the President sent his significant message, declaring that the old parties must no longer be permitted to " renew their factious struggle," and that the suffrage of the people had " adopted, not a man, but an entire system of policy," the Ministry in a body resigned.   The brief remainder of M. de Tocqueville's political life was passed in firm opposition to that " entire system."   Very happily, four years of vigour were left him for the production of a noble book—*L'Ancien Régime et la Révolution*—of which all that can here be said is, that it is more than worthy of the author of *Democracy in America*.   This work was published in 1856.   M. de Tocqueville died at Cannes on the 16th April, 1859. The political horizon was then very dark.   The institutions he loved, and to which he had been an honour, were suppressed.   The servility he hated was rampant.   But he knew that liberty has sometimes been more wisely used, and more highly valued, for its temporary loss, and that no prescription can bar the rights of a people.   He had, too, a title to console himself with the thought that in his last book he had left to his countrymen an excellent manual of political study and aspiration.   It is a legacy which the most gifted in the long and glorious line of French publicists might have been proud to bequeath.

His work on the Old Monarchy and the Revolution.

CHAPTER XI.

At the date—1846—of the entrance into the Academy of Count Alfred de Vigny,—by whose death France has just lost one of the worthiest of her men of letters,—there was already in the air, the sure signs of a coming political storm.   But those must have been keen observers, indeed, who could, as yet, anticipate a second Empire.   Still, it was again the Napoleonic ideas and the Napoleonic reminiscences that gave rise to the most notable passage of arms of a day memorable in the Academy's annals.

Etienne, De Vigny's predecessor, had been distinguished both as a journalist and as a dramatic author.   De Vigny began his speech by classifying men of letters into two main divisions—the thinkers and the improvisators.   The thinkers working for posterity ; dreading haste ; paying little regard to the hubbub around them ; aiming at perfection.   The improvisators working rapidly and impetuously for an immediate result ; studying the passing interests and tempers of the hour, both as means and as ends ; contenting themselves if they can but domineer over their contemporaries.   In the course of an animated retrospect of the life and writings of Etienne,—whom he classed, of course, with the " improvisators,"—he dwelt, with evident enjoyment, on the fortunes of a comedy, famous in its time,

called *L'Intrigante,* which had been produced, before
Napoleon himself, at Saint Cloud. He depicted the secret
disquiet which seemed to pervade society, at that epoch,
"like an epidemic." Power, he said, intoxicated with
victory and freed from all outward check, had lost its self-
control. It sought to dispose even of marriages, in accordance with political calculations and dynastic interests. Lists
of heiresses were drawn up, and too frequently an all-
powerful finger pointed to names. In Etienne's comedy,
the half-smothered discontent found expression. When
the actor—and the actor was Fleury—uttered the then
startling verses :—

De Vigny's
discourse at
his reception.

Incident in
the career of
his predeces-
sor.

> " Si je sers mon pays, si j'observe ses lois,
>   C'est à son tour l'Etat qui garantit mes droits.
>   Mon respect pour la cour a souvent éclaté,
>   Et nul n'est plus soumis à son autorité.
>   Mais que peut-elle faire à l'hymen de ma fille ?
>   Je suis sujet du prince, et roi dans ma famille :"—

the audience was excited, and the Emperor himself rose
from his seat. " The shaft had struck home. The comedy
was immediately interdicted, and the very type in which it
had been set up for the press was seized by the police."
And here De Vigny introduced a parenthetical reflection to
which subsequent events have given a but too significant
gloss :—" Thanks to the fortune of France, we are now
far removed from those strokes of absolute power, which
doubtless will never recur, and which even glory could not
excuse. The generation I belong to, which from youth
upwards has breathed no air but that of parliamentary
freedom, finds it difficult to believe that any denser atmosphere can have been tolerated."

The president of the Academy at this reception was,
again, Count Molé. Molé was then one of the very few
surviving statesmen who had held familiar intercourse with

Napoleon. He had known the Emperor in his strength and in his weakness. He had rendered good service to France, both under Napoleon and after him. By his recollections, as well as by his sympathies, he was impelled to take up the gauntlet, so boldly thrown.

Molé's view of Napoleon and his policy

In accordance with custom, a copy of the new member's intended speech had been given to the president beforehand. The MS. contained a strong metaphor about slaves and janissaries, which, in delivery, had been omitted. Count Molé, after dexterously complimenting the orator on the brilliancy of his description of scenes and events, "at which his hearers might well have supposed him to have been present," proceeded to assure him that neither M. Etienne nor he, Molé, himself, had ever been acquainted with any of those French families who had been forced to withdraw by flight from "firmans which awarded a young slave to a janissary," as the guerdon of his services. M. Etienne, he admitted, might have had reason to regret that in those days there were parents whose ambition or cupidity prompted them to marry their daughters in accordance, rather with the presumed wishes of the ruler, than with their own inclinations, but "never," he repeated, "were there, amongst us, either slaves or janissaries."

Molé then proceeded to analyse, with great ability and in a very incisive style, although from a narrow point of view, the more remarkable works of the new Academician. He dwelt especially on the limitations which the poet—in verse or in prose—ought to impose on himself, in dealing with historical events and real persons. He alleged that in *Cinq-Mars* we have veritable history drest, artistically indeed, but drest as a romance. The facts are borrowed from French annals, but there are very few facts to which the author's fertile imagination has left their identity. Had

Count Molé's criticisms on De Vigny as a Romancist.

De Vigny contented himself with resuscitating, for the
necessities of the drama, Father Joseph,—who in plain fact
died four years earlier,—and with converting into a hero
the hot-headed and presumptuous favourite, of two and
twenty, who was willing to hand France over to foreigners,
so that he might but be freed from the control of the
too-powerful Minister, it would suffice, perhaps, to ask
him whether such liberties did not put a somewhat serious
strain upon his own avowed maxim : "Truth in art"? But
why had he reduced to such mean proportions one of the
greatest statesmen of modern times? Richelieu's ambition, *His views of the character and of the ambition of Richelieu.*
in Count Molé's judgment, never had any other aim than
the power and exaltation of France.   By him, France had
been endowed with national unity, at the same time that
the royal authority had been organized on a firm basis.
Doubtless, Richelieu had too little borne in mind that
clemency is often the best counsellor of kings.   But, by
destroying the formidable powers which had vied with the
crown, he, first, had made room for the obscure, and had
subserved those plans of Divine Providence which were
already written over his head, although in a region which
his gaze could not reach.   To Count Molé's mind, such
men belong to Truth, not to Fiction.   To blend them into
romantic combinations is likely rather to dwarf them, than
to delineate.   And, finally, he reminded both Academicians
and auditory that it ought not to be thought strange if, in
the midst of a society of which Richelieu had been the
founder, a voice should be raised to recall his glory and to
defend his memory.   Whatever our estimate of the defence,
either of Napoleon or of Richelieu, it must have been
impossible to listen to this address without admiring the
vigour of the orator.   Men like Count Molé bore some
share in paving the way for Napoleon III, without quite
intending it.

CHAPTER XII.

THE COUNT DE MONTALEMBERT, AND THE ABBÉ LACORDAIRE.

UNDER the rule of Napoleon III, the Institute has been enlarged. Some details of its organization have been modified. But no change has been made—or none of importance—in the constitution of the French Academy. The most striking "receptions" have been those of the Count de Montalembert and of the Abbé Lacordaire. The former entered the Academy in 1852, within two months

The politi-
cal career of
the Count de
Montalem-
bert.

of the *Coup d'État*, and the introduction of such a man, at such a time, into the one public arena in France in which freedom of speech is, at once, a tradition of the past, and a weapon of the present, naturally excited more than usual expectation. This distinguished man had been, for a while, one of the preachers of that ephemeral gospel which sought to combine, at least a close approximation towards ultramontanism in religion, with a large measure of radicalism in politics. And, for many years, M. de Montalembert was among the most eminent and most pertinacious of the opponents of the policy of King Lewis Philip. Very early in 1848, he had foretold a Republic, and when it came, he offered it his services. His repeated contests with Victor Hugo, in the Legislative Assembly, had kept him much before the public. He had supported the restrictive laws on the press, and the expedition to Rome. In 1851, he went so far as to say that the thing France most needed was a "Roman expedition at home." And now, the thing wished for had come, although scarcely in the form anticipated.

The Academical chair on this occasion was filled by M. Guizot, whose voice, once so potent, had been unheard in public during four years. The deceased member, M. Droz, had been amongst the historians of the great Revolution, once again brought vividly before men's minds by its newest developments, and now to be, by the incoming member, vigorously arraigned and condemned in all its phases. M. de Montalembert praised his predecessor for having, under Charles X, criticised with severity the political opposition of that day, which "already was undermining the throne." He quoted, with strong approval, a passage written by M. Droz twenty-six years before:—
"When they give us the Republic, we shall have one day of liberty, and many days of tyranny—the 'liberty,' under the mob; the 'tyranny,' under some despot or other." But M. de Montalembert omitted to remind the Academy that his predecessor's name was, at that very date, recorded on one of the most honourable pages of its own history. It should not, at such a time, have been overlooked that it was not a mob that drew up the "law of Justice and Love," against which M. Droz, together with a majority of his fellow-Academicians—as much attached to wise order and good government as any Frenchmen who have ever lived— had so strenuously and so successfully protested.

His reception at the Academy.

In characterizing Droz's History of the Revolution, the orator spoke of the repeated illusions which had led men to treat the Revolution as a bygone event. "What we, like our fathers, have regarded as the entire work, was but

M. de Montalembert's summary of the Revolution of 1789.

a chapter. The Revolution has resumed its course. Once again, it has outstripped our worst fears. It has deceived alike the prudent and the bold. It has put all the fools in the right, and has given confidence to every scoundrel." With a passing allusion to certain system-mongers who had pretended to affiliate democracy upon Christianity, and to make the Revolution a Commentary on the Gospels, he proceeded to lay the whole burden of the revolutionary crimes on the Constituent Assembly of 1789. "It treated France as a conquered country. . . . By proclaiming the right of the State over Church property, it deposited in our institutions . . the germ of Communism. . . . Open the *Moniteur*, change the names and the dates; and you will find there the first editions of the doctrines which have most alarmed contemporary Europe." The Constituent, he contended, did not, indeed, abolish the monarchy, "but gave it up, disarmed, chained, degraded, with a sceptre of reed and a crown of thorns, to the executioners in the rear." This too sweeping indictment was summed up in the words :—"Let us have the courage to say it—in the face of verdicts of history and menaces of the future—the Revolution of 1789, shaping itself as it did, has been nothing but a blood-stained inutility."

M. de Montalembert's political position; and his services in other spheres of action.

More than once, and without any insincerity on his part, passing circumstances have placed M. de Montalembert in an exceptional position, and have made him appear— especially to English readers of French literature—as a combatant for opinions which he has never really held. If closely examined, his career will be found to have been substantially consistent with the principles which thirty years ago led the famous triumvirate of *L'Avenir* to visit Rome. Nor can any career better vindicate the assertion, then made by Gregory XVI to Montalembert, Lacordaire, and La Mennais, that implicit fidelity to the Papacy and consistent "liberalism" in politics cannot long cohere. But it must never be forgotten that in other than political spheres of action M. de Montalembert has rendered great and brilliant service to some of the best of social interests. Those who are old enough to call to mind the first appearance of the treatise *Du Vandalisme dans l'Art,* will ever retain a reverent love for its author, as one who fought a good fight in evil times. Those who have read, but yesterday, the eloquent and graceful *History of the Monks of the West,* will acknowledge in his latest work a substantially truthful and worthy monument raised to men who played an important part in the world, and played it well; whatever may be the difference of view between writer and readers on the great questions of the passing day, and on the degree to which monastic work and monastic aims are now but the things of a bygone time.

M. Guizot's reply was strikingly moderate and statesmanlike. He showed that it was possible to recognise at once what was truly great in the old monarchy and what was timely and useful in the governments which have succeeded it. He then glanced at the history of the Academy itself: "In paying due homage to Richelieu and Lewis XIV, it has never subjugated its thoughts, or its hopes. It regrets neither absolute power, nor the illusions of universal monarchy. I have some right to affirm that it holds Liberty of Conscience to be sacred, and deplores the Revocation of the Edict of Nantes." These words are weighty, and are in wholesome contrast with such utterances as that which was delivered, on the same spot, a few years later, when Bishop Dupanloup asserted the Clergy to be "under no obligation to Christian humility," *when* "they are defending the cause of God, *or the cause of the Church.*"

M. Guizot's Reply to M. de Montalembert.

The Abbé
Lacordaire.
Jean Baptiste Henri Lacordaire was one of four brothers, born in the first four years of the present century at Recey-sur-Ource, in the department of the Côte d'Or, all of whom have attained distinction in their several pursuits. He was educated with a view to the bar, but, after devoting two years to legal studies in Paris, with good promise of success, he became dissatisfied with the calling, and determined to enter the Church. He received priest's orders in 1827, and made his first appearance in polemical literature on the establishment, in October, 1830, of the celebrated journal *L'Avenir*.

For two years, Lacordaire, La Mennais, and Count de Montalembert, laboured zealously to preach the conjoint supremacy of the clergy in religion, and of universal suffrage in politics, through the columns of *L'Avenir*. "God and Liberty; the Pope and the People;" such was its motto. But, at the end of that period, Gregory XVI condemned these doctrines, and laid an interdict on the newspaper. The three chief writers betook themselves to Rome, and there they definitively parted company. On his return to Paris, the Abbé Lacordaire announced "his absolute submission to the Holy Father, and his determination to know no other guide than the Church; no other necessity than union; no other ambition than that of rallying around the Holy See, and the Bishops whom Divine Grace and Mercy have bestowed upon the Christians of France."

This Confession of Faith Father Lacordaire, in subsequent years, fully carried out. His many eccentricities lay on the surface. In substance, he was always the thoroughgoing but the really honest and devout advocate of the Papacy. If, on one occasion, he claimed as the distinctive boast of the Roman clergy that they "never despair of truth, of justice, and of the *liberty of the Human Race*,"* he presently illustrated his conceptions of those terms by eulogising that " Christian chivalry which took under its protection the sacred weakness of the Church," and one of the finest examples of which he recognises in Simon de Montfort, the extirpator of the Albigenses.† Dominic and Montfort, he says, " were the two heroes of the war of the Albigenses, the one as knight, the other as priest."‡ The city which witnessed some of the worst atrocities of the Inquisition ; within whose walls the Massacre of St. Bartholomew had one of its most terrible repetitions ; whose inhabitants looked on at the judicial murder of the family of Calas, in the middle of the eighteenth century ; was to the Abbé Lacordaire " like a lamp lighted by the holy doctrines of the good, the beautiful, and the noble." France, Spain, and Italy form " a sanctified zone of the world," of which zone, " Toulouse serves as a clasp," . . . " keeping in her guard, as the purest and most splendid symbol of the faith, the body of St. Thomas Aquinas."§

The heroes of the Christian Church, according to Lacordaire.

By Father Lacordaire, his Academical honours—had life been prolonged—would, probably, have been prized rather as a weapon than as a crown. There is a curious episode in one of his earlier lectures respecting Erasmus :—" You all know Erasmus, gentlemen ;—he was, in his day, the first Academician in the world. On the eve of the tempests which were to shake Europe and the Church, he wrote prose with the most consummate elasticity. All the world were at loggerheads, to obtain one of his letters. Princes were proud to correspond with him. But when the

* *Conférences de N. D. de Paris,* i, 120.
† *Vie de St. Dominique,* 65.
‡ Ib., 101.
§ *Discours pour la translation du chef de S. Thomas d'Aquin,* 42.

thundercloud burst; when it became necessary to devote oneself to error or to truth; to give, to the one or to the other, speech, glory, and blood itself; this worthy man had the courage *to remain an Academician.* He extinguished himself in Rotterdam under phrases, still very elegantly turned, but despicable."* Lacordaire was certainly in no danger of being converted into an Academician of the Erasmian stamp.

But that fiery spirit, which panted as vehemently, under the white robe of Dominic, for action and for potential influence over men's minds, as ever Simon de Montfort's had panted, beneath his steel habergeon, for warlike fame; or the keen intellect of Erasmus, under his furred gown, for scholarly predominance; was destined, like theirs, to wear out the mortal covering. Lacordaire entered the Academy in 1860. He died in 1863.

The circumstances of the Academical contest, when Lacordaire entered the Academy.

Why did the French Academy elect the author of the *Conférences de Notre Dame* to the seat which had been vacated by Alexis de Tocqueville? The answer will turn, not on the Academy's estimate of Lacordaire's literary power,—unquestionable as that was, within its narrow sphere,—but on the political, and also on the personal, circumstances of the moment. When the contest opened, the Academy had before it, as a candidate for the vacant chair, M. Henri Martin, whose *Histoire de France* it had itself crowned more than once, and whom the public had crowned, in its own pleasant way, more frequently still, by exhausting four editions of his book. It had, as another candidate, the eminent publicist and administrator, the Count de Carné, whose *Etudes sur l'Histoire du Gouverne-*

* *Le Père Lacordaire, Orateur,* article by Sainte Beuve in *Le Constitutionnel,* 31 Dec., 1849.

ment Representatif en France united literary ability with political timeliness. But it had also before it a certain M. Camille Doucet, the author of a long series of not very brilliant dramas; the historian, in a fashion, of the wars of the Empire; and the Superintendent of the department of Theatres, under the Minister of State of the Emperor Napoleon III; and M. Doucet was understood to be the Emperor's candidate. The contested seat was won, not by the accomplished Historian, or by the eminent Publicist, but by the Dominican Orator.

The Discourses, and other productions, of Lacordaire have too much savour in them to be read by any man with indifference. His own animation is so contagious that it is sure to excite either warm esteem, or vivid repugnance. No man, in our own day, has uttered sayings more true, more pregnant, more incisive, or more provokingly antagonistic to accepted and well-grounded opinions. "The great barriers of nature," he said on one occasion,—" the huge mountains, the burning sands, the trackless steppes,— prevent the world from being converted into a narrow dungeon, where nothing but steam could be breathed in freedom." On another occasion: "After a century or two from their appearance, only very few of the books, even of the great writers, are read; and, frequently, it is *the man's life* that gets his books a reading." On another, "We vanquished Arius, Mahomet, and Luther; and we founded the temporal power of the Popes. *Those are the four crowns of France.*" Of Pius IX he once said:—"When it is too late,—if it be ever too late to be just,—Italy will raise a statue *to the Washington, whom God gave her and whom she rejected!*" When he deliberately wrote:— "There is nothing in the world more hated than History, by the oppressors of the people and the enemies of God,"

The writings and the sayings of Lacordaire.

it never occurred to him that if one of his readers were, any morning, on entering his study, to take down his copies of the " Indexes, prohibitory," and of the " Indexes, expurgatory," of Lacordaire's own Church, he might quickly pen a very pithy commentary on that pithy saying.

But, with all his incoherencies, the restorer of the Dominicans in France was an honest and a loveable man. Nor is it possible to read the affectionate tribute which the Count de Montalembert has just paid—as much with the heart as with the pen—to his lifelong friend, without some echo arising to the reader's mind, and perhaps to his lips, of Lacordaire's latest prayer,—uttered in the agony of death :—"*My God! open to me; open to me.*"   We will humbly hope that that prayer has been heard.

Lacordaire's last words.

CHAPTER XIII.

THE BARON DE MONTYON AND HIS " PRIZES OF VIRTUE."—
THE GOBERT PRIZES FOR FRENCH HISTORY.

OF late years, the distribution of " Prizes" has become a prominent feature in the Academy's proceedings, mainly in consequence of the large bequests made by the Baron de Montyon, and by Baron Napoleon Gobert. In England, social nostrum-mongers, speculative tradesmen, and politicians in distress, have given very evil odour to Prize-essays. With Prizes " of Virtue" we have never yet been troubled.

Gobert's foundation seems to have been the consequence of a genuine literary ambition, weighed down by the consciousness of inadequate faculty. " I hope that I may be enabled to do with my possessions what I have not been able to do with my mind" are the words which he employs in his last Will. Intensely patriotic and proud of his country—his father had fallen at Baylen, and he was himself the godchild of Napoleon—Gobert had a burning desire to write French history. Finding that he could not do that worthily, he contented himself with endowing the Academy with valuable prizes, to be given from time to time to the authors of the best works on that subject. Augustin Thierry received from this source 9000 francs a year during sixteen years. Thierry's contributions to French history are too recent and too well known to need either estimate or enumeration at length. So long a retention of

Baron Gobert's Prizes for Works on French History.

8

Thierry's historical labours partly due to the Gobert Prizes. the chief History prize will probably be exceptional. But the exception is honourable both to the writer and to the Academy. The sixteen years during which Thierry enjoyed the prize witnessed the publication of the *Essai sur l'Histoire de la formation et des progrès du Tiers-État*, and of three successive volumes of the *Recueil des Monuments de l'Histoire du Tiers-État*, as well as of revised editions of the author's preceding and famous works. The second Gobert prize was awarded, in the first instance, to M. Bazin, for his *Histoire de Louis XIII*, and was retained by him, also, And also those of M. Henri Martin. until his death, in 1851. M. Henri Martin then obtained it for his *Histoire de France, depuis les temps les plus reculés*. In awarding this prize on behalf of the Academy, M. Villemain gave an excellent summary of the merits of the book, and concluded it by taking just exception to a phrase which Villemain on the duties of History in depicting and in estimating great men. clothes in M. Martin's words the thought of not a few writers still more widely known to fame :—" In depicting the last hours of the great and terrible Richelieu,—dying so peacefully after so many deeds of vengeance, that a pious bystander could not refrain from saying aloud, 'This is a feeling of safety which affrights me,'—the historian (whose functions this bystander had thus anticipated), shares the proud confidence of the dying man, and contents himself with the reflection :—' Apparently, these great messengers of Providence feel that they will be judged on principles which the mass of mankind cannot comprehend.' No, Sir, neither in the sight of Divine Providence, nor in the sight of that human conscience which is its noblest work, are there two orders of moral truths—two unequal systems of justice. Do not imagine that, either for a man or for a nation, there is any Dictatorship of genius or of numbers ; any mission—providential or fatal, call it which you will—that gives sanction to violence and wrong. It is to prove the contrary that we have History, and that to you has been accorded the power of writing it."

On Augustin Thierry's death, M. Henri Martin succeeded, for one year, to the first prize. The second was divided between two works—one of them being M. Chéruel's historical treatise *De l'Administration de Louis XIV.* The names of Lavallée, and of Poirson, occur among the subsequent holders of the Gobert Prizes. The Montyon endowments are partly for works of literature, partly for acts of "exemplary beneficence" and "virtue."

Antoine Jean Baptiste Robert Auget, Baron de Montyon, was born in 1733, and lived until 1820. In the course of that long life he had seen many vicissitudes. In his earlier years he had filled many distinguished offices in the Magistracy of France. He passed many years of exile in England. Possessed of a large fortune, and of wide sympathies, one of his main channels of expenditure, whether in office or in exile, consisted in acts of beneficence. In his case, charity was not posthumous, but life-long.

As early as 1780, he established, in the French Academy, an annual prize of 1200 francs for that work, published during the year preceding each adjudication, which "should seem most conducive to the temporal well-being of mankind." In this, and some other like endowments, he invested a capital of 60,000 francs, which was confiscated in the Revolution, and which he subsequently himself replaced. At his death, in 1820, he bequeathed to the Academy a further sum of 20,000 francs, yearly, for ever— one half to be employed in the reward of publications "useful to morals" (*utiles aux mœurs*); the other, in the reward of virtuous and exemplary deeds. He established other prizes, under the guardianship of the Institute, for the encouragement of scientific researches and of sanitary improvements, with which I do not here concern myself. And he further bestowed on the Institute an interest in his residuary estate.

In the administration of the literary prizes, the Academy has aimed at the encouragement of such works, of indisputable and high utility, as yet, from their subjects and character, are little likely to bring pecuniary return to their authors. Works on psychology, on ethics, on social economy, on education, on the history of literature, appear in the list of books rewarded, and among the names of their authors are some of the best names of the last and present generations.

Prizes for "deeds of virtue" trench obviously on very dangerous ground, but in administering them the Academy seems to have displayed remarkable discretion and wisdom. Montyon's gifts have been made to soothe the closing hours of many lives, the vigour of which had been spent in acts of self-devotion—sometimes in acts of lofty though obscure heroism—brought at length into light by no effort of the doers. By judicious management, and wise restriction, the publicity of such rewards,—which might easily have become an evil,—has been made the means of much good.

The beneficent prizes of Count de Maillé Latour Landry.

Every literature has its Chatterton, and every time that the story is vividly retold, or its closing scene depicted once again by a painter of genius, seed is sown which is likely somewhere or other to bear good fruit. The two best known examples, in France, of the untimely nipping of youthful intellect, are linked together both in French poetry and in the annals of French beneficence. The author who wrote, in a public hospital, the famous verses :—

" Au banquet de la vie, infortuné convive,
J'apparus un jour, et je meurs," &c.,

had previously written, *La faim mit au tombeau Malfilâtre ignoré;* and in the Will of Count de Maillé Latour
Landry, the stories of Gilbert and of Malfilâtre, are mentioned expressly as among the motives which induced the
testator to bequeath to the French Academy, and to the
Academy of Fine Arts, 30,000 francs, the interest of which
is to be given every alternate year, "to some young writer
or artist, poor in circumstances, whose "evident talent and
promise may seem to deserve encouragement to pursue its
career, either in letters or in the arts." The administration of this bequest is judiciously left to the Academies,
in turn, without the publication of their acts, but on their
proper responsibility.

CHAPTER XIV.

SUCH seem to me to be a few of the chief personages and of the more notable incidents which lie scattered amongst the yet uncollected annals of an institution, to which almost every great writer in France, for more than two centuries, has been proud of belonging. Other actors and other incidents may, possibly, have as good a claim to record as those which I have chosen. But enough has been said to vindicate my assertion that in the discussions, the rivalries, the public receptions, and the public rewards, of the French Academy, there lie vivid reflections of those varying aims and tendencies in a great national literature, which mark epochs in the intellectual history of the world at large.

Retrospective glances at the Academy's career.

Within that small arena, the mind of France may be seen both in its weakness and in its vigour. When Richelieu's institution was yet in its cradle, inflated and indiscriminating panegyrics, vapid verses, acrostics on the fine eyes of Clelia, or sonnets on Dorinda's dimples,—intermingled with moral essays, in prose of exceeding dullness,—are the staple products. For a time, Lewis the Great, Lewis the Good, even Lewis the Beautiful, is, in the Academic pæans,

sung to all sorts of tunes, until the stock resources of
diction and metaphor are exhausted, and the praise can but
repeat itself :—

> "Trope nods at trope; each figure has a brother,
> And half the *Eloge* just reflects the other,"

But, very soon, themes of weight and pregnancy take the
place of these puerilities, and are treated worthily. A
series of clear and comprehensive appreciations of the
Worthies of France, of all classes,—Poets, Warriors, Statesmen, Writers, Inventors,—stimulates those budding intellects which, in some happy instances, will ripen into the
Worthies of a generation to come. The Academy might
fairly boast that within its walls the real glory of the
Nation began to outshine whatever there was of mere
tinsel in the old Monarchy. Prosperous Ministers and
haughty Prelates had there, at times, to listen to useful and
homely truths. The best intellects of an eminently intellectual people were there exerted in honouring, alike the
achievements of the greatest minds of France, and deeds
of humble self-devotion performed by French peasants.
Nowhere have the duties of men of letters, as well as their
claims,—the responsibilities as well as the glories of the
Pen,—been dwelt upon more impressively than in the hall
of the French Institute, the head-quarters of a Literature
to which (despite the flood of foulness which has more than
once swept over the track of Fenelon and of Racine, of
Pascal and of Bossuet) nations near and remote—Englishmen and Americans, Scandinavians and Spaniards,—will
ever lie under deep intellectual indebtedness.

Such traditions are onerous. In recent years the Academy has shown that it can resist both imperial frowns
and imperial flatteries. It has repeatedly asserted the

What such a career involves.

liberty of thought and the freedom of speech which elsewhere seemed, for the time, to have been stricken down.
But, in its choice of weapons, it has not always, I think,
kept its history in mind. It has sometimes chosen, both
for vacant seats and for a temporary leadership, men with
minute claims to literary honours, but gifted with fluent
and unscrupulous tongues,—men likely to prove thorns to
the hand of power, but little likely to augment the trophies
of French intellect.

The public responsibilities, and perhaps the moral influence, of the French Academy, were never greater than now.
That influence is not less real, because it is often unseen.
To brilliant services, and to great memories, the Academy
adds a certain prestige of durable vitality which, in France,
has become rare. When Richelieu founded it, there stood
side by side with the new society, many institutions that
seemed to have quite as good a chance of long life. But
most of these have been either suppressed or revolutionized.
The names may sometimes be the same, but the institutions
which bear them are very different. The Academy itself
has undergone several changes of mere form and routine,
but it is substantially unchanged. Here, long before
1789, men of the "privileged orders" had to become the
supplicants, before they could become the associates, of other
men whose claims to distinction were quite independent
of birth or of wealth. It is, indeed, alike the honour, the
safety, and the great advantage, of the Academy—as it has
also been of other institutions, and of other countries,—
that among its men of genius there have always existed men
of high birth, as well as men of lowliest origin. But with
their Academical seats, the accidents of fortune had, essen-
tially, nothing to do. And here, in 1864,—if Parisian
gossip may be accredited,—the Emperor Napoleon III,

The Aca-
demy's dura-
bility, and
substantial
unity.

unsatisfied with that official protectorship of the Academy which adheres to the throne, as well as undeterred by the cutting sarcasms which Mr. Kinglake has recently levelled at him as "a sallow-faced man of letters," is a candidate for admission, by the votes of an absolute majority of his future colleagues. The assert-ed candida-ture of the Emperor Na-poleon III

Even at the election of April, 1863, occasioned by the death of Duke Pasquier, some pressure (it is asserted) was, in the first instance, put upon the Academy in order to induce it to delay its choice, in order to introduce, with befitting pomp, the imperial candidate. It seems to have been thought that the long-promised *Vie de César*, might possibly have been forthcoming in time to form a firmer pedestal for literary honours than the *Idées Napoléoniennes*, the treatise *Du Passé et de l'Avenir de l'Artillerie*, and the *Rêveries Politiques*. The formal candidature which on that occasion was withheld, has since, it is said, been authoritatively announced.

The reception of Napoleon III, as "one of the Forty of the French Academy," come when it may, will be a sight worth seeing. It will be as strange an event, in its way, as was the imperial visit to London in 1852, or the imperial entry into Milan in 1859. It will now, indeed, lack one circumstance which is said to have had its special charm in the Emperor's own imagination, and which could not but have been impressive to all spectators. Pasquier had been in office, under the old Monarchy, prior to the Convention of the Notables. He had served Napoleon, in several prominent offices, from the Consulate down to the close of the first Empire. Under the restored Bourbons, he had taken a large part both in making ministries and in over-turning them. He had been the most intimate and most trusted counsellor of Louis Philippe. He had presided · Career of Pasquier, one of the lately deceased Aca-demicians.

over that long series of political trials, which fills a place
so unfortunately conspicuous in the annals of the citizen-
kingship, and includes the trial of a famous "con-
spirator," once captured at Boulogne. In a word, the
public career which had begun before the Revolution of
1789, had continued up to the eve of the Revolution of
1848.

It could not but have been a memorable thing to have
seen Pasquier's chair taken by the heir of Napoleon,—the
President of the Republic,—the successful plotter of
December, 1851—the consummately able ruler of France,
—the half-unwilling liberator of Italy. By Academic usage,
the new member must epitomize the qualities and the
career of his predecessor ; the president of the day, those of
the new member. Completeness or impartiality in such an
epitome is, of course, as little desired as it is expected. But
there is no want of Academic precedent for plain speaking,
or hard hitting. To have heard—with whatever inevitable
reticences and suppressions—the salient features of two
such careers, and of two such characters, passed in elaborate
review, the one series by Napoleon III, and the other series
by a Montalembert or a Guizot, would have been to see
history unrolled before one's eyes as in a living panorama.

This is now a bygone possibility. If, however, the imperial candidate should enter the Academy as the successor
of Alfred de Vigny, the piquancy of the scene to those of
the beholders who may chance to remember that remarkable
reception of De Vigny himself, in 1846, which has been
already described, will be scarcely less. Whatever its date
or circumstances, the Emperor's reception into the French
Institute—if that be indeed among the "surprises" which
the Future has yet in store for us—cannot fail to be a sight
worth beholding.

The imperial candidature is, by no means, the only circumstance which has given adventitious interest to the
recent Academical Elections in Paris.   Bishop Dupanloup, The recent
pamphlet of
Bishop
Dupanloup.
of Orleans, has thought the occasion a fitting one for a
zealous attempt to make theological orthodoxy one of the
conditions precedent, which must henceforth be united in
the persons of all candidates for the "blue riband" of
French Literature.

There is no denying the duty, or the necessity, of some
regard to the moral and social qualities, as well as to the
literary powers, of aspirants to that eminent distinction.
But morality, and a lofty aim in life, is one thing, and
orthodoxy, after the pattern of the Roman Church, quite
another thing.   There never was a time when,—in France,
as elsewhere,—the need for the inculcation, and the enforce-
ment by example, of high aims in literature, has been more
obvious.   The rapid growth of the merely industrial and
material interests of society, and the wide diffusion of the
bare rudiments of learning, have combined to supply a
new gloss to the text of the old complaints.   A paradoxical,
inflated, and enervating, literature more than keeps its
place beside the honest, pure, and healthful, literature.   It takes advantage of the multiplied means and
agencies of modern mechanism, and modern publicity, and
needs to be encountered by every legitimate influence of an
opposite tendency.   The very language which the illustrious
writers of three centuries have ennobled, is daily corrupted
and trampled into the mire.   Here lies the true field for
Academic exertion and example.   It is idle to attempt to
transport the Confessional into the Institute of France.

Among the Candidates of April, 1863, was M. Littré, a
contributor of many brilliant articles to the *Revue des deux
Mondes,*—one of the continuators of the *Histoire Littéraire*

de France, of the Benedictines,—one of the Editors of the *Journal des Savans,*—and the author of an elaborate *Dictionnaire Etymologique de la Langue Française,* now, after a labour of some eighteen or twenty years, in course of publication. But M. Littré is also a zealous follower of Auguste Comte,—an untiring advocate and expounder of the so-called " Philosophy of Positivism."

That "Philosophy" is sufficiently, and very obviously, open to criticism. But, at this date, it ought to be quite needless to argue, with a body like the French Academy, in favour of freedom of opinion. Life is too short for the constant iteration of rudimentary propositions. It might, surely, now be taken as settled that Truth as little needs the aid of social stigma or of social penalty, inflicted on its opponents, as it needs the aid of prize or bounty-money, conferred upon its friends.

The " *Avertissement aux Pères de Famille* " is believed to have had some share in bringing about the rejection of M. Littré, and the election of M. de Carné, his opponent. Of their relative claims, as authors, little need be said. The personal question is of small moment, in comparison with the question of principle. All that M. Dupanloup has to urge on that point, he seems to sum up in these words :—" It is puerile to suppose that I have any such power [*i. e.,* the power of exclusion from the Academy], but, if I had it, I would unhesitatingly use it, simply because I esteem the Academy very highly ; because I look upon it as a raised platform, whence doctrines descend with loud resonance ; because I cannot see with satisfaction the proselytism of error obtain consecration, and lift itself to such an eminence."* If teaching like this had governed the Academy in past days, it would have been shorn of its

* *Avertissement, &c.,* p. 11.

honours. It has become a power in France by acting on
a quite different doctrine. Its past history has made it an
object of reverence to the lovers of literature in other
countries, just because that history records repeated
examples of its efforts on the side of free thought,—free
speech,—free examination ; and of its successful vindication
of the vital doctrine that the real interests of Truth, and the
wise policy of a nation, alike demand that assertion shall
be met by inquiry, and argument by argument.

In April, 1863, all the candidates possessed some literary
reputation, although in very different proportions. The
successful candidates, M. Dufaure and M. de Carné, are
eminent publicists. With both of them, literature is
simply the handmaid of politics. Scarcely any thing has proceeded from the pen of either which has not, in some degree,
a political aim. The imperial candidature stands apart. It
is, at all events, a significant and a timely tribute to the
potencies of thought. It is in curious contrast with the
imperial disdain of "ideologists" and "phrasemakers,". so
often asserted—more asserted, perhaps, than felt—during
the first Empire. It may, possibly, be another indication
that a policy in flagrant conflict with the best intellects of
the day is already seen to be a policy which, sooner or
later, must suffer extensive change. But in such candidates
as M. Littré (candidates whose claims rest on books) the
keenest opponent, if an honest one, can hardly fail to
recognize pretensions which are in obvious harmony with
the thing aspired to. Such men present examples of brilliant and varied literary attainments, in union with eminent
services rendered to that particular branch of learning
which the Academy is, by its very charter, especially
bound to promote, and with a lifelong devotion to Litera-

The com-
parative
claims of the
Candidates of
1863.

ture, for the love of it. I humbly venture to think that
whenever it honours such a career the French Academy
honours itself. It is, in such cases, at once acting in
accordance with its own best precedents, and is practically
rebuking a fanaticism, from the dominance of which no
interests would suffer more . than the interests of good
letters. And the interests of Literature in France are the
interests of remote readers, all over the world.

II.

THE EARLY BIOGRAPHERS OF KING ALFRED.
WITH SOME ACCOUNT OF AN UNPRINTED
CHRONICLE AND CHARTULARY COMPILED,
AT WINCHESTER, IN THE FOURTEENTH
CENTURY.

BEHOLD a pupil of the Monkish gown,
The pious ALFRED, King to Justice dear!
Lord of the harp and liberating spear;
Mirror of Princes! Indigent Renown
Might range the starry ether for a crown
Equal to his deserts, who, like the year,
Pours forth his bounty; like the day doth cheer,
And awes like night with mercy-tempered frown.
Ease from this noble miser of his time
No moment steals; pain narrows not his cares.
Though small his kingdom as a spark or gem,
Of ALFRED boasts remote Jerusalem,
And Christian India, through her widespread clime,
In sacred converse gifts with Alfred shares.

Ecclesiastical Sonnets, I, xxvi.

CHAPTER I.

1. SEVERAL of the Roman Catholic Historians of our early Church,—and more especially such as wrote either towards the close of the sixteenth century, or in the earlier part of the seventeenth,—quote a MS. Winchester Chronicle, the existence or the fate of which have since been unknown. Some of the passages seem to point to similarity of source, as well as of subject, with the well-known Chronicle of Thomas Rudborne,* printed by Wharton, in 1691, in the first volume of the *Anglia Sacra.* But it is seen, on glancing at the latter, that the quotations are not from Rudborne, and that the discrepancies between the printed Chronicler and the manuscript Chronicler are much greater than the resemblances.

2. The titles under which this MS. Chronicle are quoted differ. Michael Alford, in his elaborate *Annales Ecclesiæ Anglicanæ*, cites it repeatedly as *Annales Cœnobii Wintoniensis (e. g.* Tom. III, pp. 161, 164, 165, 204, 206, 208, 209, &c.). Nicholas Harpsfeld, the author of the

(marginal note: Quotations from the Book of Hyde in Romanist Historians.)*

---

* "Ecclesiæ Wintoniensis Historiam fusè præ aliis digessit Thomas Rudburn, Ecclesiæ ejusdem Monachus. Novi Monasterii Wintoniensis, quod ab Hidâ nomen accepit, fuisse monachum Baleus malè tradidit. Ecclesiæ enim Cathedralis S. Switheni cœnobitam fuisse, tum ex plurimis *Historiæ Majoris* locis, tum ex Prologo ad *Historiam Minoeem* liquet· Balei errorem Pitsius et Vossius transcripserunt," &c. WHARTON, ut supra. I. 26.

Historia Anglicana Ecclesiastica printed at Douay, in 1622,
quotes it, sometimes (*e.g.* p. 159), as *Annales Novi Cœnobii
Wintoniensis,* sometimes merely as *Annales Wintonienses.*
Hugh De Cressy, again, in his *Church History of Brittany*
(p. 776), having to speak of a certain oration made by the
Abbot Grimbald—the friend of King Alfred—at a Council
convened in London, in the year 886, writes thus:—"If
the reader have the curiosity to peruse the whole Oration,
he must have recourse to the fore-mentioned *Annals of
Winchester,* or the book called *Liber de Hida,* where it
hath been preserved in a gratefull memory of St. Grimbald."
I doubt, however, if Cressy had ever seen the MS. he cites.
Much of his book is a translation and compilation from
Alford. It was completed in France. And there is reason
to think that his knowledge of *The Book of Hyde,* as of
other English MSS. quoted in his History, was at second
hand.   Both Alford and Harpsfeld had passed long years
of study in English libraries and in English country
houses.

John Stow's
partial Epi-
tome of the
Book of Hyde.
3. But the traditional knowledge of this Hyde MS. did
not rest simply on its quotation by our earlier Church
Historians.   Good and diligent old John Stow,—among
his other and multitudinous labours,—came across it, in
August, 1572, and transcribed rather more than a third of
its contents.   One is sorry to observe, on looking at this
unfinished transcript—now preserved, as No. 717 of the
Lansdowne MSS., in the British Museum — that to
him paper must have been even scantier than leisure.
Apparently to save paper, Stow has made his copy in such
a cramped, abridged, and mutilated fashion, that in many
places it is unintelligible.   And, to increase the difficulty
arising from this source, when the transcript came to be
bound, its leaves were confusedly intermingled by the binder.

From both causes, together, the learned and able editor of *The Church Historians of England*, Mr. Joseph Stevenson, when he included an English translation of Stow's fragment in the fourth volume of that useful publication, fell into several grave mistakes,—which no amount of Editorial acuteness, indeed, could have averted, in the absence of all access to the original MS.

4. That long-lost text I had the satisfaction of discovering, in 1861, in the Library of the Earl of Macclesfield, at Shirburn Castle in Oxfordshire. It is on vellum; of large folio size—$17\frac{3}{8}$ inches by $11\frac{3}{4}$ inches—written in double columns; has, on some pages, richly illuminated borders and initial letters; and extends to 78 pages, or 156 columns, with 58 lines to each column. It breaks off in the middle of a sentence, and indeed of a word, but, from the circumstance that on the later pages the initials and other embellishments are sometimes only sketched in outline, and sometimes not even sketched, but only indicated by the pen, it seems probable that the MS. was never completed by the scribe. It is, perhaps, not so much—in the usual sense—imperfect, as unfinished. The Binding is only of the earlier part of the 18th century. Other particulars of the age and character of the book will be best exhibited by fac-similes. The historians who have quoted it, and the antiquary who transcribed its earlier chapters, are alike silent as to its local habitation, when seen by them respectively. The MS. itself contains nothing to indicate through whose hands, or into what libraries, it may have passed.

Discovery of the Macclesfield MS. at Shirburn Castle.

5. Those who care to learn anything of the history of the Library in which the book was discovered, will find a statement of what is known on that point in a subsequent portion of the present volume. Here, it may suffice

to mention (first) that the Shirburn library combines the books of two English Collectors of the end of the seventeenth century and beginning of the eighteenth,—namely, Thomas Parker, first Earl of Macclesfield, and Lord Chancellor; and William Jones, F.R.S., the friend and occasionally the amanuensis of Newton;—and also a large selection of the choicest books of that ardent lover of fine books the French publicist Nicholas Joseph Foucault, whose life has just been narrated by M. Baudry; and (secondly) that the growth of the Shirburn Library, by successive bequests to former Earls of Macclesfield, had rendered some of its best books inaccessible until the present Earl directed the writer to re-arrange it, in 1860-61.

6. Stow, although he says not a word about the place or ownership of the MS. which he partially transcribed in 1572, has twice given a sort of vague description of the book. In the sixth volume of that portion of his MS. "Historical Collections" which is preserved among the HARLEIAN MSS. (No. 542, p. 123) he writes thus :—

Stow's descriptions of the appearance and contents of the Book of Hyde.

"*Annales Monasterii de Hyde* is an auncyent booke conteynynge the orygynalls and encrease of that howse wth the notable thyngs that hapned there. It sheweth the author that wrote it lyved about the yere . . ," but the date is a blank.

Again, at the end of the fragmentary transcript already described (LANSDOWNE MS., No. 717) he writes :—

"Memorandum, that there be in the booke of Hide, in greate and large parchment writen, dyvars of thes things before writen, and many other testaments of certeyn Saxon kings, which be writen in bastard Saxon, and translated into latyn and englysshe."

Mr. Hardy's account of Stow's transcript.

7. The most eminent of living English antiquaries—*facile princeps* as respects the field of labour we are now concerned with—Mr. T. Duffus Hardy, Assistant-Keeper of the Public Records, after examining Stow's fragment, wrote thus: "The Book of Hyde . . . is a reconstruction of earlier materials, ... compiled within that monastery, and thus contains details—especially respecting Alfred and his contemporaries,—not elsewhere to be found. . . . It contains citations of authors whose works have perished, and who are known only by this manuscript, and by the Chronicle of Thomas Rudborne which has much in common with the *Liber de Hida*. . . . . . No MS. copy is known but that of John Stow."

8. Here, it may not be inappropriate to add that the words "which has much in common with the *Liber de Hida*," apply—as they were in fact applied—rather to the Lansdowne fragment, than to the Macclesfield MS. In like manner, a remark made by Mr. Stevenson, that "the Book of Hyde in many respects corresponds closely with Asser's Life of King Alfred" must be taken in a very limited sense. What the precise extent of this resemblance is will be seen presently. Meanwhile, it suffices to record the fact that, whatever the relevancy of Mr. Stevenson's remark as regards Chapters XII and XIII of the Book of Hyde, as it appears in the Macclesfield MS., that remark has no bearing, whatever, on the other twenty-one chapters.

Account of the contents of the Book of Hyde.

9. The Macclesfield MS. has no title. It commences, at the top of the recto of the first leaf with the words :—

"*Regnum quod modo Anglia noīatur olī* [nominatur, olim] *dicebatur Albyon. et hoc modo. Ut enim repperi in quadam cronica vetustissima qd* [quod]

fuit in regno syrie qidam [quidam] *rex nobilis noīe*
[nomine] *Dioclitianus,"* etc.

10. Beginning with the old story of Labana, the first
chapter closes with a summary of English history until the
Norman conquest. Chapters II to VIII, inclusive, describe
individually each of the kingdoms which composed the
Saxon Heptarchy. The ninth chapter is devoted to those
Saxon kings who relinquished their earthly empire, and
gave themselves to the especial service of Heaven, by embrac-
ing a monastic life. The tenth chapter answers the question,
Whence was the origin of those Saxons who reigned in
England? The eleventh is entitled " *De Monarchis," (i.e.*
" Of the *sole* monarchs.") Thenceforward, each chapter is
the Chronicle of a single reign—" *Cronica Regis Adulphi;"*
—" *Cronica Regis Alfredi ;"*—and so on. But, after the
thirteenth,—the Chronicle of Alfred—although the division
into chapters virtually continues, both the designation and
the number are discontinued. The Macclesfield MS.
breaks off abruptly in the middle of the " *Cronica Regis
Cnutonis,"* [C. XXIII] in the middle of a sentence; and in
the middle of the ancient name of the see of Hexham,
thus :—

    " *Cnutone regnū* [regnum], *anglor* [anglorum]
tenente, alfricus wyntoniensis ecclīe [ecclesiæ] *preposi-
tus assumitur in presulatū* [præsulatum] *Eboracensis
eccliæ* [ecclesiæ]. *Hiis primū* [primum] *queritur
cōtra* [contra] *dunelmiū* [dunelmium] *epm* [episcopum]
Edmundū [Edmundum] *quo jure ipe* [ipse] *hangus."*

The illuminated initials and other decorations cease to
be entirely and uniformly finished, with the recto of the
seventeenth leaf. Some exceptions occur, here and there,

but speaking generally, the ornamentation of the MS., from the verso of leaf 17, onwards, is in various stages of incompleteness.

11. Each chapter or "chronicle," from the thirteenth to the twenty-first inclusive, but with the exception of that devoted to the short life of St. Edward, King and Martyr, is followed by an appendix of Charters, Wills and other documents, relating, more or less directly, to grants of land and other benefactions conferred on the Monastery of Hyde. The wills; the descriptions of boundaries; sometimes—as in the instance of the very curious narrative of the "Crimes and forfeitures of Wulfbold," and of the severe courses taken with him by King Ethelred and his magnates at a grand Council convened in London,—a portion of the proem prefixed to the grants, are given in Anglo-Saxon (usually in a very corrupt and uncouth orthography) and in middle English, as well as in Latin. In most cases, such portions of the documents exhibited as are given in the three languages, are given with equal fulness in each language. In the case of the Narrative relating to the unhappy Wulfbold, the Latin is only an abridgement. Of these documents, however, a fuller account will be given in a subsequent chapter. And one of them—previously known to antiquaries—will be quoted at length, for the sake of its curious English version.

CHAPTER II.

RELATIVE STATUS OF THE EARLIER HISTORIANS OF ALFRED.
—HARMONY OF THE CHIEF EVENTS IN HIS LIFE, AS
NARRATED (1) IN THE *SAXON CHRONICLE;* (2) IN THE
ANNALS ASCRIBED TO ASSER, OF ST. DAVID'S; (3) IN *THE
BOOK OF HYDE ABBEY.*

1. On a multitude of questions connected with the age,
the authorship, the genuineness, the variations of style, and
the preferable text, of the SAXON CHRONICLE, antiquaries
have been as much divided in opinion, as were those two
knights who, meeting at a cross-road, fought about the

Character of the Saxon Chronicle.

real colour of the famous shield. But on the one point,
that in the Saxon Chronicle we have substantially the
earliest historical account of Alfred, competent opinions
may be regarded as agreed. It seems, also, to be tolerably
well settled that, whoever may have been the writer of those
passages which relate to the closing years of Alfred's life,
the writer was contemporary with our venerated king.

2. Scarcely less conflicting, than the debates about the
Saxon Chronicle, have been the opinions of our antiquaries
as to the sources, the authenticity, and the historical value,
of the Annals of the Exploits of Alfred, ascribed to Asser.
The latest—and certainly not the least able—of the modern

Character of the work ascribed to Asser.

biographers of Alfred, Dr. Pauli, inclines to accept Asser
as substantially genuine. His learned and accomplished
translator, Mr. Thomas Wright, on the other hand, is quite

certain that the Life of Alfred attributed to Asser, " *cannot*
have been written before the end of the tenth century, and
was probably the work of some monk who, with no great
knowledge of history, collected . . . . the traditions relating
to Alfred which were then current; joined with them the
legends in the Life of St. Neot, and the historical entries
in the Saxon Chronicle; and to give greater" [appearance
of?] "authenticity to his work, published it under the
name of Asser." The weighty fact that Lingard, Hardy,
Kemble, Thorpe, Lappenberg, and Stevenson,—as well as
Pauli,—take the other side, very happily delivers the
present writer from all temptation to the presumption of
offering any opinion, of his own, on so vexed a question.

3. Asser ceased to narrate the exploits of Alfred at or
about the year 890. Alfred lived until 901. Asser is
found attesting charters in 904.* According to the *Annales
Cambriæ*, he survived until 908; according to the Saxon
Chronicle, until 910. Why did he so abruptly break off
in his self-imposed and most honourable task? The question, at present, and so far as any endeavours of mine at
its solution are concerned, admits of no reply. There are
more difficulties in the way of the hypothesis that we have
lost some portion of what Asser left, than there are in the
way of the other and—under this point of view—the more
awkward hypothesis, that what we actually have includes
interpolations, and additions, which Asser never saw.

4. No ancient MS. of Asser is now known to exist. All
that can be usefully stated as to his sources, and as to his
text, has been briefly but sufficiently summed up by Mr.
Stevenson, in his able "Preface to Asser" in the fourth
part of "The Church Historians of England" (1854), to
which I refer the reader.

* Kemble, *Codex Diplomaticus Ævi Saxonici*, No. 437, &c.

Other early
Biographers
of Alfred.

5. Ethelwerd, " the Patrician," wrote towards the close of the tenth century. His work is in substance a mere compilation from the Saxon Chronicle, but from a copy, or, so to speak, a re-cast, of that Chronicle, which has perished. Ethelwerd, therefore, though a copyist, is, in a sense, an authority. Florence of Worcester seems to be a copyist, and nothing more. His respect for the Saxon Chronicle, and for Asser, is so great that he copies them textually, whilst his modesty, also, is so great that he lays no claim to their acquaintance. He is also much indebted to that general chronicler, Marianus Scotus, whose labours have so often been laid under contribution. Henry, Archdeacon of Huntingdon, who compiled his Chronicle at the beginning of the twelfth century, abridges the earlier historians, and occasionally adds information obtained elsewhere. The Chronicle which goes by the name of " John of Wallingford " largely follows Huntingdon; incorporates with its extracts numerous legends of saints; and seems to have been compiled about the middle of the twelfth century. But of its real authorship, the most competent inquirers are quite uncertain. Simeon, of Durham, in addition to the contributions he has levied on his earlier fellow-chroniclers, has much matter of his own. He was the contemporary both of Florence and of Henry Huntingdon. Finally, another contemporary of those historians, William of Malmesbury,—the author of the universally-known works *De gestis Regum Angliæ*, and *De gestis Pontificum*— has contributed an item or two to our knowledge of Alfred and of his times, although "England's darling" had probably rested from his labours some hundred and seventy years, when Malmesbury was born.

6. The *Liber de Hida*—so far as concerns the parentage, the life, and the reign of Alfred—confines its express

quotations from early chroniclers—and those quotations are
of little importance—to Florence of Worcester, and to
Henry of Huntingdon. But it quotes largely the *Policroni-
con* of Ralph of Chester ; the lost treatise of Vigilantius, *De
Basilica Petri;* the lost *Epistola ad Monachos Nigros in
Anglia* of Bonagratia de Villa Dei ; and the lost books of
Gerard of Cornwall, *De gestis Regum Westsaxonum.*

7. For the purposes of this little Essay it will suffice to
compare,—with the utmost possible brevity,—the principal
events in Alfred's life which it narrates, with the correspond-
ing statements in the Saxon Chronicle, and in Asser. And
the columnar form will best exhibit both the agreement
and the diversities existing between the old authorities
and the new one. I translate the Latin of the Book of
Hyde, as it stands in the Macclesfield MS., and quote the
other writers, in the existing versions, nearly as I find
them :—

[849.]   In the year 849 was born Ælfred......
in the royal vill which is called Wanating, in
......Berrocscire.

[853.]   Æthelwulf sent his son Ælfred to
Rome, with an honourable escort, both of nobles
and commoners. .... Pope Leo ....
anointed for king the aforesaid child Ælfred,
and confirmed him, receiving him as his son of
adoption.

[855.]   In the same year, he went to Rome
with much honour, taking with him his son
Alfred......... because he loved him more than
his other sons, and remained there a whole year.
....
" In this place I think it right to relate as
much as has come to my knowledge, about the
character of my revered Lord Alfred, ...
during the years in which he was an infant and
a boy. .... As he advanced through
the years of infancy and youth, his form appeared
more comely than that of his brothers ; in look,
in speech, and in manners he was more graceful
than they.   His noble nature implanted in him,
from his cradle, a love of wisdom above all
things ; but, with shame be it spoken, by the
unworthy neglect of his parents and nurses, he
remained illiterate even till he was twelve years
old or more ; but he listened with serious attention to the Saxon poems, which he often heard
recited, and easily retained them in his tenacious
memory.   He was a zealous practiser of hunting,
in all its branches, and pursued that art with
great assiduity and success. ....

A.D. 853-855.	SAXON CHRONICLE.	A.D. 853-855.	BOOK OF HYDE ABBEY. (MACCLESFIELD MS.)

[The Saxon Chronicle notices no event in the Life of Alfred prior to his first visit to Rome, usually ascribed to the year 853.]

[853.] K. Æthelwulf sent his son Ælfred to Rome. Leo was then Pope of Rome, and he consecrated him king, and took him for his son at confirmation.

[853.] Alfred, because he was more beloved by his father than the rest of his sons, was sent to Pope Leo V [sic for IV]. The Pope, at his father's request, received him with great honour and caused him to be anointed King of the English.

[855.] Æthelwulf went to Rome in great state, and dwelt there twelve months.

[855.] The most religious king Athulf, not long afterwards,—namely in the year following that in which his anointed son Alfred had returned to England from Rome,—again took him thither,...........and there remained with him a whole year ....

....

"He also sent his most Christian son (beloved with pre-eminent affection,* but already assailed by an incurable disease) to be healed by St. Modewenna, who was then living in Ireland..............................

King Etheldred was dearly beloved, above the rest of his brothers, by the most illustrious prince Alfred, on account of his eminent virtues which daily increased. And hence, Alfred, the skilful leader and general in arms, often opposed himself to the Danes, at the walls of

* "Regalem indolem plus ceteris dilectam."

" On a certain day his mother was showing him and his brothers a Saxon book of poetry, which she held in her hand, and said, ' Whichever of you shall soonest learn this volume, shall have it for his own.' Stimulated by these words, or rather by a divine inspiration, and allured by the beautifully illuminated letter at the beginning of the volume, he answered, before any of his brothers—his seniors in age, but not in grace—' Will you really give that book to him who can first learn to understand it, and to repeat it to you ?' His mother smiled, and confirmed her promise ....In due time, he had learnt and he recited, his task. After this, he learned ' the daily course,' that is, the celebration of the Hours, and afterwards certain Psalms and Prayers .... But, sad to say! he was unable to gratify his most ardent wish to acquire the liberal arts, ... for lack of teachers. ....When he was more advanced in life, he was harassed by so many diseases, unknown to all the physicians of this island, as well as by the internal and external anxieties of sovereignty, and by the continual invasions of the Pagans, and' had his teachers and writers, also, so much disturbed, that there was no time for reading. But yet among the impediments of such a life, from infancy up to this present time, and, as I believe, even until his death, he continued to feel the same insatiable desire of knowledge, and still aspires after it."

SAXON CHRONICLE.	A.D. 855.	BOOK OF HYDE ABBEY (MACCLESFIELD MS.)
		Wilton,* in defence of that leader of a holy life, King Etheldred. .... Thus, King Alfred, most renowned among a thousand, came of the nation of the Britons, and thus of the noble blood of the Trojans. After he had passed his twelfth year he committed to memory, like a teachable child, the Saxon poems. In hunting, he was eminent. In architecture, supreme. The Psalms and Prayers he collected into one volume which he called 'Manual,' that is a Handbook, and carried always about him. In grammar he was less skilled, because at that time, there was not any teacher of grammar in the kingdom. For this reason, and by the advice of Abbot Neot, whom he frequently visited, he established public schools of various arts, which in many points brought advantage to the city [?]. For Alfred, the bountiful Almsgiver, the most devout worshipper at mass, the most studious searcher-out of unknown arts, called to his Court the most holy confessor Grimbald from France,—a monk skilled in literature and in music,—together with the priest and monk John, a man of sharpest intellect and universal learning, and with the venerable Asser, a man profoundly versed in literature. He also in-

* . . . . " Wyltoniensium murū contra danos se opposuit, &c."

[868.] Alfred, at that time occupying a sub-
ordinate station, asked and obtained in marriage
a noble Mercian lady, daughter of Ethelred,
surnamed Mucil ("The Big"), Earl of the Gaini.
.... Ethered and Alfred ....
went with an immense army, and entering
Mercia came to Nottingham, eager for battle
.... but the Mercians and the Pagans
made peace, and the brothers returned home.
....

[871.]...Ethered and Alfred united their forces,
and approached Reading with their combined
armies. When they had come to the gate of the
citadel they cut down all the Pagans whom they
found on the outside ....
.... At Ashdown ['Aescesdun'] ....
the Christians, like the Pagans, divided their
forces into two bodies .... Alfred march-
ed up to the battlefield promptly with his
followers, as we have heard it related by
truthtelling eye-witnesses. His brother, King
Ethered, remained at prayer in his tent, hearing
mass, distinctly affirming that he would not depart alive before the priest had finished the service. ....Alfred, ...when he could
no longer sustain the assault of the foe, unless
he either retreated .... or rushed on, ...
without waiting for his brother, ... relying
on God's assistance, drew up his men in a
dense body and advanced. .... At
length, when both armies had struggled with

A.D. 868-871.	SAXON CHRONICLE.	A.D. 871.	BOOK OF HYDE ABBEY (MACCLESFIELD MS.).

[868.] Æthered and Ælfred ... went with the West-Saxon power into Mercia, as far as Nottingham ... but there was no great battle, and the Mercians made peace.

vited John, a monk, from the farthest parts of Wales, namely from the Monastery of St. Davids, that he might instruct the nobles in learning.......

[871.] ...... About three days after, King Æthered and Ælfred his brother led a large force to Reading, ... and there was great slaughter made on either hand .... And .... after this, King Æthered, and Ælfred his brother, fought against the whole [Pagan] Army at Æscesdun. .... Ælfred fought against the division under the earls............... .... Fourteen days after, Æthered and Ælfred fought ... at Basing, but the Danes conquered. .... And two months after, they fought against the army at Meretun. And, after Easter, King Æthered died. .... Ælfred succeeded, and, about one month after, fought against the Danes at Wilton, and put them to

[871.] .... At Ashdown, constrained by necessity, Alfred gave battle before King Ethelred his brother, then attending mass, was ready..................The Christians, led by Alfred, climbing the hill, slew Osrith, king of the Danes, with five of the enemy's generals and many soldiers, and pursued the remnant, all day, as far as Reading. .... Ethelred, whom the glorious prince Alfred had forced to reign before himself, died .... leaving his kingdom to his dearly-loved brother.

K. Alfred, most devout in Christian faith and piety, fourth in order of birth, who while his brothers reigned was always in a secondary station, succeeded after Ethelred—best loved in the concordant

A.D. 871.	ASSER.

extraordinary courage and fierceness, the Pagans, through the Divine justice, ... and after the slaughter of the greatest part of them, fled disgracefully. One of their two kings, and five chiefs, perished. .... Fourteen days after, Ethered and his brother united their forces and advanced towards Basing, ... and triumphed.

After Easter, in the same year, K. Ethered went the way of all flesh. .... Alfred, who up to that time ...... had only held secondary rank, undertook the government of the whole realm. ....

And, when one month had elapsed, he fought a very severe battle against the whole force of the Pagans, on a hill called Wilton .... But the Pagans deceived their over-sanguine pursuers, returned to the battle and claimed the victory.................

Besides this, there were endless skirmishes, both by day and night, in which Alfred was often engaged...

* "Alfredus, princeps in fide et religione xpiana vigilantissimus, qrtus natu, qui regnantibus fratribus semper fuerat secondarius, post Etheldredum, in unicordie fraternalis armariolo predilectum, ad integram monarchiam Westsaxonie successit."

[The reader who may have inclination and opportunity to look at the translation of Stow's fragment, as given in *The Church Historians of*

SAXON CHRONICLE.	A.D. 871-874.	BOOK OF HYDE ABBEY (MACCLESFIELD MS.).
flight for a good part of the day.		brotherly breast—to the sole monarchy of the West Saxons, &c.*... .... This glorious Prince had a battle with the Danes at Wilton, in which both armies were in great peril. And so in the first year of his reign he fought with the Danes nine times in the open field.......
		[874.] In the third year he made peace with them. But in one night they killed all his cavalry. The great king pursued them to Exeter.........

England, will see that the many imperfections and confusions of that fragment have led even so experienced and accomplished an editor as Mr. Stevenson into several mistakes. Of these mistakes, and also of many omissions—even in that part of the "Book of Hyde" which is professedly given,—Stow's illegibility and haste are obviously the cause; as will be perceived, at a glance, if the Lansdowne MS., No. 717, be itself referred to.]

[875.] .... Alfred fought a naval battle
against six pagan vessels and took one of them,
whilst the rest escaped.

....

[876.] .... K. Alfred entered into
a solemn covenant with the Pagan army, on
condition that they should depart, ... giving
him such hostages as he chose. They also swore
an oath on all the relics .... that they
would immediately leave his realm. .... But,
acting falsely, they broke the treaty, ... and
slew all the cavalry around the King.............

[877.] .... King Alfred ordered boats
and galleys to be built throughout the realm,
.... and in these he placed expert seamen
to guard the approach by sea. He himself
hastened to Exeter, ... and besieged the
Pagans within that city........................
At Suanavic [Swanwich] in the same year, a
hundred and twenty of their ships perished, while
K. Alfred pursued their cavalry to Exeter
where he [again] received hostages.

A.D. 875-877. SAXON CHRONICLE.	A.D. 877. BOOK OF HYDE ABBEY (MACCLESFIELD MS.).
[875.] .... In the Summer, Ælfred went out to sea with a fleet, and fought against the forces of seven ships. One of them he took, and put the rest to flight.	
[876.] .... Afterwards the King made peace, and the Pagans gave to him hostages, and swore oaths to him on the holy ring.	
[877.] K. Ælfred with his forces rode after the [Pagan] Army as far as Exeter.................... Their fleet was overtaken by a great storm and a hundred and twenty of their ships were wrecked at Swanawic. .... They delivered hostages to Alfred and then observed the peace. .... [878.] Ælfred, with a small band, retired with difficulty to the woods and the moors. .... And after this, at Easter, constructed a fortress at Æthelney, ... and rode to Ecgbyrth's-stane. .... and to Ethandune, and there fought against the whole [Pagan] army and put them to flight .... and that army delivered	[877.] In the sixth year of his reign, ... the Danes, sailing from Wareham towards Exeter, lost a hundred and twenty vessels in a storm at sea .... Alfred passed a precarious and restless life in the woods of Somersetshire, for he had nothing to live upon, save what he caught by fowling, by fishing, or by hunting............... [Then follows the story of the vision of St. Cuthbert.] " Encouraged by the admonitions of St. Cuthbert, the King issued from his covert ; .... and, in the garb of a minstrel, entered the tents of the Danish King, and thence, having explored them, returned to Ethelingey. .... And, presently, overthrew his foes, by sudden onset, with great slaughter. ... With

[878.] .... In that year, Alfred,
with a few of his nobles and soldiers, passed a
restless life in much anxiety among the wood-
lands and marshes of the County of Somerset.
.... As we read in the Life of St.
Neot, he was long concealed in the dwelling of
one of his own cowherds. .... [*Then follows
the well-known story of the country housewife and
the cakes, and also the famous passage on the in-
firmities and the affliction of the King.*]

K. Alfred formed a citadel in a place called
"Æthelingaeg," whence he made ceaseless as-
saults upon the Pagans .... and, in
the seventh week after Easter, he rode to
Accgbryht's-stone [Brixton-Deverel? in Wilts],
in the Eastern part of Selwood ....
and thence .... removed his standard
to Ethandune [Edington], where he contended
in close phalanx against all the Pagan forces
.... and, by Divine aid, won the victory,
.... and pursued the enemy with great
slaughter..........................

"Godrum," their king .... he received,
at a place called Alre, near Æthelingaeg, as his
adopted son, and raised him from the sacred
font. His chrism-loosing took place at the royal
vill called Waedmor. .... And
King Alfred bountifully gave him many excellent dwellings...........................

A.D. 878.	SAXON CHRONICLE.	A.D. 878.	BOOK OF HYDE ABBEY (MACCLESFIELD MS.).

hostages to him, with many oaths.
....

[878.] And the King was God-father to "Guthrum" at baptism .... at Aulre, and his chrism-loosing was at Wedmore; .... and Ælfred greatly honoured him with gifts. ....

the help of the people of Wilts, Somerset, and Hants, he built a citadel at Ethelingey (" the Island of Nobles"), whence, rushing on the enemy, he repeatedly overthrew them. At length, receiving hostages, he took their king, "Gutrus," to the font with twenty of his best men, and gave to him the name of Athelstan. .... But the Ethiop cannot easily change his skin. .... Gutrus remained a tyrant for twelve years. .... He was succeeded by a Dane named Echric. ....

....

Alfred, like a second Mattathias, ... fought, in one year, nine battles against the Danes, and at last the victory, through Divine Providence, remained with him. .... But the provinces which that renowned prince had given to the Danish king to dwell in, not to govern, ... threw off their allegiance, when "Gurmund" rebelled against his spiritual father; and thus Alfred, like his brother Ethelred, lost, by his own goodness, that sole Monarchy of all England, which throughout his life he could never recover.

[882.] In this year, Alfred fought a naval battle, ... and captured two of the Pagan ships...................

A.D. 882-883.	SAXON CHRONICLE.	A.D. 881-883.	BOOK OF HYDE ABBEY (MACCLESFIELD MS.).

SAXON CHRONICLE.

[882.] Ælfred went out with his ships and fought against the Danes, and took two of their ships.........

[883.] That same year, Sighelm and Æthelstan carried to Rome the alms which the King had vowed to send thither, and also to India, to St. Thomas and St. Bartholomew, when he sat down against the army at London.................and largely obtained the object of his prayer. ....And Marinus

BOOK OF HYDE ABBEY (MACCLESFIELD MS.).

[881 ?] In the same year, on the death of Bishop Tunbert, Alfred appointed Dunewulph to the see of Winchester. Discovering the natural talent of the man whilst he was yet a swineherd, he sent him, though advanced in life, to be instructed in learning. Never did Alfred allow any unlettered person to acquire rank in the Church. .... Alfred then repaired Septonia, which is Shaftesbury ;................. received from Pope Martin [Martin II, 882—884] a large piece of the Cross ; .... and, in the seventh year of his reign, ... compelled the Danes to raise the siege of Rochester. .... In the same year, he repaired London, ... and entrusted the keeping of it to Ethelred, Earl of the Mercians......... ....

[883.] About this time the illustrious king sent his alms to Rome and to India, and built two monastries, at Ethelingesye and at Shaftesbury. ....
On a certain day, while the Danes were pressing hard upon him, he refused to leave the Church in which he was hearing Mass, until

ASSER.

A.D. 883.	SAXON CHRONICLE.	A.D. 883.	BOOK OF HYDE ABBEY (MACCLESFIELD MS.).

the Pope sent "Lignum Domini" to K. Ælfred.

the service was over, ... but as soon as it was finished he joined combat with the Danes, slew their king, Oseg, with a lance, and the king's son with his sword. Many other of the Danish leaders fell there, and the victory remained with King Alfred.

Many more battles did he fight,—which it would take too long to narrate,—for the Danes allowed him no breathing time. .... But at length he reduced them to subjection. ....

This Alfred promulgated most excellent laws. .... He used always to carry in his bosom a Psalter, so that whenever he might chance to have leisure he could take it out to read. .... The rebelliousness of the flesh at that time caused him much disgust............... But he used to contemplate the examples of the Saints, that he might drive away temptation, beseeching God to chasten his flesh with some infirmity, if it might please Him not to render the king wholly unfit for the government of his kingdom. And, for many years, Divine Providence caused him to suffer from the disease called "ficus". .... On which account, despairing of cure, he went into Cornwall, to the Church of St.

[884.] To the succour of Rochester, Alfred arrived with a large army............... Then, the Pagans fled hastily to their ships .... and were so hotly pursued that they returned to France the same summer. ....
Pope Martin sent many presents to the aforesaid King, among which was no small part of that sacred and venerable Cross on which Our Lord was suspended, for the salvation of all mankind. ....

In the same year the Pagan force disgracefully violated the peace which they had made with K. Alfred..............................

[*Then follows the long digression on Alfred's character, sickness, and piety; and on the personal intercourse which Asser had held with him.*]
....

[886.] Alfred handsomely rebuilt the city of London, made it habitable, and entrusted it to the care of his son-in-law, Æthered, Earl of Mercia...................

["In the same year, an injurious and distressing discord arose at Oxford."]....................

Here follows the famous passage alleged to have been interpolated by Camden;—of which hereafter.]

A.D. 885.	SAXON CHRONICLE.	A.D. 883.	BOOK OF HYDE ABBEY (MACCLESFIELD MS.)
			Guerour. .... But a much more serious illness seized him, even on his Wedding-day, and continued from his twentieth until his sixty-fifth [*Sic* in MS. for *forty*-fifth.] year............................. ....
	[885 ?] The townsmen defended Rochester till Ælfred came with his forces.		
	That same year Ælfred sent a fleet to East Anglia .... and they captured the ships of the pirates ; but, as they returned home, with their booty, a large fleet of pirates fought against them and had the victory.		
	[885.] The Pagan army broke the peace made with Ælfred		
	[886.] Ælfred repaired London, and all the English submitted themselves to him except those who were in bondage to the Danes.		

A.D. 887.	ASSER.	

[887.]   In this year K. Alfred began to read and to interpret, all at once, on the same day, by a Divine instinct. ....
....
....
....

. This king was pierced with many nails of tribulation, although invested with royal authority.
....
And was harassed by the constant invasions which left him no interval of repose. ....
....
....

He founded two monasteries, ... and endowed them amply. ....
....

[*Then follow the passages on the division of his revenues, and the employment of his time.*]

A.D. 887-901. SAXON CHRONICLE.	A.D. 900. BOOK OF HYDE ABBEY. (MACCLESFIELD MS.).
[887.] Alderman Æthelhelm carried the alms of......... K. Ælfred to Rome.............	
[888.] Alderman Beocca carried the alms of............ K. Ælfred to Rome...............	
[894.] K. Ælfred ....gathered together his forces, and fought against the Pagans at Farnham, ...and put their army to flight............... But those who dwelt among the Northumbrians and the East Anglians gathered ships ; .... and besieged a fortress in Devonshire...... ....When the King heard that, he turned westward towards Exeter, ... and of the Danes there was great slaughter...............................	
[896.] Ælfred commanded long ships to be built to oppose the 'æscas' of the Danes.	[900]. .... In the last year of his reign, this most benignant of sovereigns first avowed to Holy Grimbald his determination to build a monastery in Winchester, but, prevented by death, the most pious king was unable [in person] to fulfil his vow.............................. ....
[901.] In this year died Ælfred, six days before All-hallowmass.	

These passages I am obliged both to abridge and to select. But they will, I think, suffice to justify the assertion that in the Chronicle of Hyde we have an authority which, in some important particulars, is both independent and interesting.

The interest would doubtless be materially increased if the comparison were carried far enough to show what is the precise bearing of the new matter contained in this Chronicle,—concerning the early history of Oxford and the life and influence of St. Grimbald,—upon the old and much-controverted question as to the authenticity of that famous passage in Asser, which has led to a perhaps too-confident aspersion upon the venerable name of Camden. This will need to be done, but it cannot satisfactorily be dealt with now.

Hereafter, too, it may be possible to show that the Book of Hyde Abbey—in respect as well of its defects, and confused chronology, as of its sources and general character— has a wider bearing on other questions which relate to Alfred's biography and early biographers. I will hope that I may be enabled by and bye to submit the Chronicle, in its entirety, to the examination of more competent antiquaries. I have already, by the kind permission of the Earl of Macclesfield, completed a transcript of it.

CHAPTER III.

LIST OF THE AUTHORITIES QUOTED BY THE HYDE CHRONICLER.

THE following is a complete List of the Authorities—
in the order of the first occurrence of each of them —
which are avowedly quoted in *Liber de Hyda*, as it appears
in the Macclesfield MS. :—

1. RALPH [HIGDEN] of Chester, *Polychronicon :*
   Book I, c. 9, Story of Brutus, &c.
   ,, V, c. 39, The sending of Alfred to Modewenna, in
   Ireland.
   ,, VI, c. 1—6, The Life of Alfred, generally.
   ,, ,, c. 7, Bones of Galfredus, &c., at Glastonbury.
   ,, ,, c. 8, Death and Character of Edwy, &c.
   ,, ,, c. 12, Murder and burial of Edward the Martyr.
   ,, ,, c. 13, Childhood of Ethelred.
   ,, ,, c. 16, Sack of Canterbury by the Danes.

2. VINCENTIUS, *Speculum Historiale :*
   P. 4. " Brutus and Marcomannus."

3. VIGILANTIUS, *De Basilica Petri :*
   C. 8, Conversion of Ethelwold.
   ,, 9, Council at Winchester ("vocal crucifix") [Twice
   quoted].
   ,, 15, Monkhood of Athulf or Ethelwulf.

4. ALFRED ("Treasurer of Beverley," ALUREDUS *Bever-*
   liacensis), *Chronica :*
   Egbert's Conquest of Essex.
   Life of St. Dunstan.
   Death of Edmund the Elder.
   Edmund Ironside—Battle of Scearstan.

11

5. " *Cronicantes Regnum Orientalium Saxonum :*"
   Pagan Kings of Essex.

6. BEDA, " *De gestis Anglorum :*"
   " I.   c. 29." Conversion of Sibert (K. of Essex).
   " III. c. 17."   „   Peada
   " V.   c. 7." Ceadwalla.—whether monk or not ?
   .. *ad finem*. Account of his own works.

7. RALPH *de Diceto* (Archdeacon of London) :
   Foundation of Westminster Abbey.

8. " FLORENTIUS, *Florarium Historiale :*"
   IV, c. 16, Burning of Cambridge.

9. ISIDORUS. *Etymologia :*
   IX, " Germania."

10. WILLIAM of Malmesbury, *De Regibus :*
    I, Egbert " monarch ;" Beda.
    II.   „   in France.
    .. Expulsion of the Seculars.
    .. Athelstan's war with Constantine of Scotland.
    „ Verses on Athelstan.
    .. Imprisonment and Release of Abp. Ulfstan.
    .. Coronation of Edwy, &c.
    „ Death of Edwy.
    „ Edgar's legislation on drinking " *ad mensuram*."
    .. Death of Edward the Elder ; Murder and Burial of
       Edward, K. and Martyr ; Baptism and Childhood of
       Ethelred.

11. WILLIAM of Malmesbury, *De Pontificibus :*
    II, Removal and Reburial of the body of St. Elphege.
    IV, Maiolus at Clnny.

12. BONAGRATIA (*de Villa Dei*), *Epistola ad Monachos
    Nigros in Anglia.*
    Monkhood of Athulf.

13. LANTFREDUS, *Vita Sancti Swithini :*
    I, Prosa nona. [Printed in Migne, *Patrologiæ Cursus,*
       Tom. CLV, pp. 62, seqq.]

14. MARIANUS *Scotus, Chronica :*

    I, c. 15, Education of the Children of Edward the Elder.
           Gift of Fragments of the Holy Cross to Malmesbury.
    II,   Victories of Edmund over the Danes.
    ..   Death of Edmund.
    .,   Comparison of Edwy and Edgar (" Good and bad
           plants growing on the same soil.")
    ..   Establishment and Reformation of Monasteries by
           Edgar.
    ..   Suppression of Robbers.
    ..   Battle of Scearstan.

15. GERARD of Cornwall [Girardus, *Cornubiensis*].   *De Gestis Regum Westsaxonum :*

    C. 10, 11, 14, Life of Alfred.
    V, c. 10, Schools at Cambridge, founded by Edward the
        Elder,
    XI, Combat of Guy of Warwick and Colbrand the Dane.

16. HENRY of Huntingdon :
    V, Verses on Alfred.

17. *Vita Sancti Athelwoldi,* c. 10.

18. An Anonymous versifier on Athelstan.

19. JOANNES, *Historia Aurea :*

    Establishment of Monks at Winchester, and at Thorney,
        under Edgar [Twice quoted].
    Account of Beda.

20. SENECA :
    " Gallus in proprio sterquilinio."

21. *Vita Sancti Eleuti :*
    Dream of Edgar.

22. An Anonymous versifier on Edgar.

23. " OSDUERUS," *Vita Sancti Dunstani.*

24. MATTHEW *Paris :*
    Battle of Penn.
    Battle of Scearstan.

25. [ROGER of Wendover.] *Flores Historiarum.*
    Reign and Murder of Edmund Ironside.
    Events in the reign of Canute.

26. *Liber de Gestis Pontificum Dunelmensium :*
    Election and Life of Bp. Edmund.
    Honours paid to St. Cuthbert by Canute.
    Account of Beda.

27. " Libello *De Vita Venerabilis Bedæ.*"

28. *Legenda Sanctorum :*
    On the Origin of the Epithet " Venerabilis Beda."

29. *Vita Sancti Birini :*
    [Quoted, but not expressly named.]

30. *Vita Sancti Cuthberti.*

Of these authorities, the *Speculum Historiale* of Vincentius; the work *De Basilica Petri,* of Vigilantius; the *Epistola* of Bonagratia; the *Historia Aurea;* and nearly the whole of Gerard of Cornwall, *De Gestis Regum West-saxonum,* together with the work cited as " *Cronicantes Regnum Orientalium Saxonum,*" are not now known to exist. And even as respects mere citation, but little more is known about any of them, than may be gathered from the passages quoted in the Chronicle of Hyde, and in the *Historia Major Wintoniensis,* of Thomas Rudborne.

CHAPTER IV.

CONCERNING THE DOCUMENTS EXHIBITED IN THE HYDE
CHARTULARY.—TEXT OF KING ALFRED'S WILL IN ANGLO-
SAXON AND IN MIDDLE ENGLISH.

THE Wills given in this Chartulary are those of (1)
King Alfred; (2) Elfsige, a Bishop; (3) King Edred; (4)
Athelwold, one of the Officers of King Ethelred II; (5)
Athelmar, a "Duke" or military leader under Ethelred II.
All of them are given in Latin, in Anglo-Saxon, and in
Middle English.

The Charters, or portions of Charters, conveying grants
of lands to Hyde Abbey,—or to persons who afterwards
gave or bequeathed the possessions first granted to them
to that Community,—are twenty-five in number. They
are the Grants of Edward the Elder, of Athelstan, of
Edred, of Edwy, of Edgar, and of Ethelred II. The
boundaries of the lands granted (as I have already mentioned,) are uniformly given in the three languages, severally.
In the proems we meet with Greek words, such as "cosmi,"
" protoplastos," and the like, which,—as Mr. Kemble has
long since pointed out in the preface to his invaluable
Codex Diplomaticus Ævi Saxonici,—are in perfect keeping
with the style of the tenth century, although very suspi-
cious if met with in documents claiming to be of a date
anterior to Alfred. The " sanctions," too, are uniformly of
the kind usual at the period. The date of the indiction is

commonly given, and is sometimes accompanied by the dominical year. In the "teste," the uncouth use of Anglo-Saxon characters in writing Latin words is also common. Most of the lands granted are situated either in Hampshire, in Surrey, or in Sussex. Kent occurs but rarely.

King Alfred's Will.

Of the famous Will of King Alfred, no MS. was accessible to Mr. Kemble, notwithstanding his wide-spread researches. Manning had printed it, in 1788, from a MS. then belonging to Mr. Astle, afterwards preserved in the Duke of Buckingham's Library at Stowe, and now, it is believed, in the rich collection of Lord Ashburnham, but he failed to obtain a sight of the MS. itself. He therefore printed after Manning's text, as the only alternative.

In the text of this Will, as given in the Macclesfield MS. of the Chronicle and Chartulary of Hyde, there are many obvious corruptions. The Will itself is treated as two separate documents, which are divided by a portion of the Chronicle. The orthography is very corrupt. In writing compound words, the particles are often separated, in a fashion more than usually uncouth. But I think it best to copy—as literally as may be—the MS., as it stands before me.

"Incipit Testamentum Alfredi Regis Incliti in lingua Saxonica :"

"First Will" of King Alfred, in Anglo-Saxon.

"Ic Aelfred cinge, mid goddes gyfe and mid getheahtunge Aeþeredes ercebisceopes and ealra Westseaxena witena gewittenesse, smeade ymbe minre sawle thearfe, and ymbe min yrfe thaet me god and min ildran for-geafon, and ymbe that yrfe thaet Athulf cinge, min faeder, us thrim gebrotherun becuaethe, Ethelbolde and Etherede and me, and swyle ure swyle lengest waere,

thaet se fenge to eallum; ac hit ge-lamp thaet Athelbolde
gefore, ꞇ wyt Aethered, mid ealre Westseaxena wytena
gewittenesse uncurne dael othe-faestan Ethelbirt cinge
uncrum maege; on tha ge-raedene the he hit eft ge-dyde
unc swa ge-wylde swa hit tha waes, tha wit hit him othe-
faestan, ꞇ he tha swa dyde, ge thaet yrfe, ga thaet he mid
uncrum ge-manan be-geat ꞇ thaet he sylf gestrynde.
Tha hit swa ge-lamp thaet Ethered to fenge, tha baed ic
hine, be-foran urum witum eallum, thaet wit thaet yrfe
gedaeldon ꞇ he me a-geafe minne dael, tha saede he me
thaet he naht eathe ne mihte to-daelon, for-thon he
haefde ful oft aer on-ge-fangen ꞇ he cuaethe thaes the
he on uncrum ge-manan ge-bruce ꞇ gestrynde, aeftyr his
daege he namum menn sel ne uthe thonne me ꞇ ic thaes
tha waes wel ge-thafa. Ac hit ge-lamp thaet we ealle on
haethenum folce ge-brocude waeron; tha spraece wit
ymbe uncre bearn, thaet hy sumre áre be-thorftan, saelde
unc on tham brocum swa unc saeld, tha waeron we on
gemote aet Swinbeorgum; tha ge-cpaedon wit on Westseaxena witena gewittenesse thaet swather uncer leng
waere, thaet he ge-uthe otheres bearnum thara landa the
wit sylfe begeaton, ꞇ thara land the unc Aethulf cinge
forgeaf be Athelbold lifiendum, butan tham the us thrim
gebrotherum ge-cuaethe; ꞇ thaes uncer aegther othrum
his wedd sealde swather uncer leng lifede, thaet se fenge
aegether ge to land ge to madumnu[1] ꞇ to eallum his
aehtum, butan tham daele the uncer ge-whaether his
bearmunn[2] becpaed. Ac hit gelamp thaet Ethered cinge
ge-for, tha ne epdde me nanan mannum[3] nanan yrfe-ge-
wryt, ne nane gewittenesse, thaet hit aenig other waere
butan swa hit on gewittenesse aer ge-cpaedon, tha ge-
hyrde we nu manegu yrfe-geflitu: nu tha laedde ic Aethulfes
cinges yrfe-ge-writ on ure gemot aet Laugan-dene ꞇ hit
man a-raedde be forane eallum Westseaxena witum. That[4]
hit a-raedde waes, tha baed ic hy ealle, for minre lufan ꞇ
him mine wedd bead that ic hyra naefre maenne[5] ne on-

[1] Madumum (Manning's text).   [2] Bearnum.   [3] Nan mann.
[4] Tha.   [5] Naenne.

cuthe for-thon the by on riht spraecon, ꝺ thae hira nanne[1]
wandode, ne for minan lufan ne for minan[2] aege, thaet hy
thaet folc-riht arehton ; thylaes aenge[3] man cucthe thaet
ic min maeege-cyld, otthe yldran otthe gingran, mid tho
fordemde, and hy tha calla to riht gerehton ꝺ cuedon that
hy nane rihtre riht ge-thecan ne myhtan ne on tham yrfe-
gewrite ge-hyran : nu hit eall agan is thaer on[4] othe thyn
hand, thon thu it be-cuethe ꝺ sylle swa ge-sibre handa
swa fremdre, swaether the leofre sy : ꝺ hy calle me thaes
hyra weodd scaldon ꝺ hyra hand setene, that be hyra life
hit naenge mannan naefre waende[5] on nane other wisan,
butan swa swa ic hit sylf ge-cuaethe aet tham nyhstan
daege."

(2) In Middle English.

" I Alfred westsaxene kyng thorw goddys gyft and by
the ordenawns of Ethered Erchebyschop, and of alle
westsaxene nobylte, wytenesse be they schull of the intent
for my sowle powerte of the herytage that god and my
prycys have y gyfe me, and of the herytage that Athulf
kyng my fadyr us thre bretheryn be qweythyd, Athelbold,
and Ethered, and me, that ho of us the wyche lengist
lyvyd schold have all the kyngdom.   And yf hyt happe
that Ethelbold fyrst be dede, than Ethered, wyht all the
nobylte of westsexene to be wyttenesse of owr partye the
tyme of Ethelbyrt kyngys coronation w[t] all owr power
aftyr the sewerte that he made to us that he so wolde
hyt be as hyt was when he hyt knew to fore the tyme of
hys coronacyon, whan he hys sewerte made of the herytage
the whyche he w[t] owre help and men getyth and that
wherto is bore, and hyt so happyd that Ethered fenge to
the kyngdome tho bade y hym be fore all owre wyttenesse
that he know te heritage to departe, and he to gyfe me

---

[1]   Thaet hyra nan ne.   [2] Minum.   [3] Aenig.
[4] On daeron.   [5] Naenig man naefre ne onwende.

my part. Tho seyd he to me that he naw3t scholde ne
my3t hyt departe for so myche that he hyt so long holl hath
y holde, but he seyde thus that the londys that he thorow
help of owre pepyll hat gete and the lyfelode that he was
bore to, to no man aftyr hys day to have and for to
rejoyse, hys herytage take wolde but onlyche to me. And
tho was y wel plesyd. And yf hyt happyd that we alle
were had and take to hethyn folke; than knowe we to
ordeyne for owre chyldryn that evereyche of hem my3t
aftyr other take owre londys and to rejoyse as they were
take to us. We therfore gaderyd at Swymborn, where
we seyden in knowleche of alle Westsaxene lordys that
they ber wytnesse that wheyther of us lenger lyfe, that
he be qweythe otherys chyldryn tho londis that we owre
sylf gate and tho londis that kyng adulpf us yafe by
Ethelboldys lyfday, wᵗ owte that the wheche to us thre
bretheryn he be qwethyd. And so of us eythyr other
hys sewerte that whether of us lenger lyved that he foug
to otherys lond and lordschyp, and to all hys good,
wᵗ owte that part that eyther of us otherys chyld be
qweythyd, and hyt so happe that Ethered kyng dye before
me, than wᵗ owte me ys no man none eyre by wrytynge
ne by no wytnesse that euy other were wᵗ owte that he
hyt by wyttenesse the rathyr sey : Tho y hyrde that my
kynnys folke was passed owt of the wordele, so than was y
Kyng Athulphys eyr thorw wrytynge and owre cownseyl
at Langdene. And a man hyt redde by fore wyttenesse
of alle Westsexene. When hyt redde was tho comawndyd
y hem all for my lofe and to hem y made sewrte that y
nevyr hyrde of man ne of coude that of my lyflode eny
ryth claymyd and that y nevyr hyrd contrarye. And no
man for my lofe nother for myn hatered sey a yens ryth
nother untrewthe sey that y my cosynnys chyld olde or
yonge not desheryte. And they alle to the ryth consentyd
and seyden that they knew no rythtyr eyer nother be
thenke coude ne mythte no other of othyr eyr here eny
wrytynge but of me ; now thw hast hyt all a yen in thyn
hond, now beqwethe hyt and yyf (*sic*) hyt to thy next kyn
or frend, whether the lefyst ys. And they all to me here

sewerte made and w^t here honde a seled that by here lyf
nevyr hyt to eny man nother other wyse torne nother
ʒyfe but so as y my self hyt be qwethe at the nexte
day."

" INCIPIT SECUNDUM TESTAMENTUM ALFREDI REGIS INCLITI, IN
LINGUA SAXONICA :——

₁ All these documents are here given, *literally*, as they appear in
the Macclesfield MS.

" Ic Alfred Ƿestseaxena cinge mid godes gife ꞇ mid
þisse ge-þittenesse ge-cþeðe hu ic ymbe min yyfe æftest[1]
minum dæge. ærnest ic an Eadpearde minan yldrian suna
þese landes æt stræatneat on truconscipe, ꞇ heoritig tunes,
ꞇ þa boc-land ealle þe Leof-heah hylt ꞇ þ land æt carumtune, ꞇ æt cylfantune, ꞇ æt burinhamme ꞇ æt pebmori ; ꞇ ic
com fyrimðig to þam hipum æt ceobrie þ hy hine ceosan
on þa geriað þepe æri ge-cþeben hæfðon mid þam lanð æt
ciptune ꞇ þam þe þæri to hyriað, ꞇ ic him an þæs lanðes
æt cantuctune ꞇ æt bedemdan ꞇ æt fefesige[2] ꞇ hysseburi
nan ꞇ æt suttune ꞇ æt leobruban ꞇ æt apeltune. ꞇ ealle þa
boclanð þe ic on cent habbe ꞇ æt þam nyðerian hysseburinan ꞇ æt cyselbene agyfe man in to þintanceastrie
on þa geriað þ hit min fæberi æri ge-cyeðe, ꞇ þ um
sundori-feoh[3] þæt ic egulfe oð fæste on þam neoðerian
hysseburinan. ꞇ þan ginʒrian minan suna þa lanð æt
eaðerungtune ꞇ þ æt bene ꞇ þ æt meone ꞇ æt ambries
byriʒ ꞇ æt beone ꞇ æt sturie mynsteri ꞇ æt gifle ꞇ æt
crunærin ꞇ æt hpitan cyrucan ꞇ æt axanmuðan ꞇ æt
bruincæscumbe ꞇ æt columtune ꞇ æt tpyfiriðe ꞇ æt mylen-
burnan ꞇ æt exanmynsteri ꞇ æt suðespyriðe ꞇ æt liptune ꞇ
þa lanð þe þeri to hyrian, þ sinð ealle þe ic on pealcyne
hæbbe butan truconstirie. ꞇ minrie yldstan ðehteri þæne
ham æt pelepe, ꞇ þærie mebemestan æt cleariari ꞇ æt
cenðeferi, ꞇ þærie ʒinʒestan þone ham æt pelʒ ꞇ æt

---

[1] Yrfe wille æfter (Manning's text).   [2] Beeewinban ꞇ at Pefesigge.

[3] Fæðer ær geewæð. ꞇ ðæt min sunðerfeoh.

æschune¹ ⁊ æt cippanhamme, ⁊ æðelme mines brioðeri
suna þonc ham æt ealbing hurinan² ⁊ æt cumtune ⁊ æt
crumbellan ⁊ æt beabinȝū ⁊ æt beabinȝa hamme ⁊ æt
burinham ⁊ æt þunresfelba ⁊ æt æscenȝum ; ⁊ aþelpolbe
mines brioðori ˌ suna þone hamme æt ȝobelminȝum ⁊ æt
ȝilbeforiba ⁊ æt stæningū, ⁊ osferiðc minum mæge þone
ham æt beccaulea ⁊ æt hþiyðeriam felba ⁊ æt biccanlinȝum
⁊ æt suðtune ⁊ æt lullinge minsteri ⁊ æt anȝemærinȝum
⁊ æt felh hamme ⁊ þa lanb þe þæri to hyrian, ⁊ ealhspiðc
þone ham æt lambburinam ⁊ æt panetinȝ ⁊ æt cðanbunc,
⁊ minnum tpan sunum an þusenb punba, æȝðrium fif hunb
punba, ⁊ minrie ylbstan behteri ⁊ þærie mibemestan ⁊
þærie ȝinȝstan ⁊ ealhspiðe, him feopium, feopeþ hunb punba
ælcum an hunb punba, ⁊ rompa ealboþ-manna elcum
an hunb manȝcusa, ⁊ æþelme ⁊ aðelpolbe ⁊ osfeþðe
eac spa, ⁊ æþeþebe ealboþmenn anb speopbon hunb
teontiȝum mancusum, ⁊ þam mannum þe me folȝiað þe ic
nu on easteþ-tiðum feoh sealbe tpa hunb puuba agife
man him ⁊ bæle man him be-tpeoh ælcum spa him to ge-
byrian pille æfteþ þæpe pisan þe luc him nu bæle³, ⁊ þam
epce-bisceope c. mancusa, ⁊ esne bisceop ⁊ peþfeþðe
bisceope ⁊ þam æt scireburnam, eac spa ge-bæle foþ me ⁊
foþ min fæbeþ ⁊ foþ þa fscynb⁴ (sic) þe he foþe þingobe
⁊ ic foþe þingie, tpa hnnb punba, fiftig mæsse-pþeostoun
ofeþ eall min juce, fiftig eaþmum goðef (sic) þeopum, fiftig
eaþmum peaþfum, fiftig to þæþe cyþucan þe ic æt þest, ⁊
ic nat naht gepislice hpæðeþ þæþ feoþ spa micel iþ, ne ic
nat þeah hiþ maþe sy butan spa ic pene. Gif hit maþe sy
beo hit him eallum gemene þe ic feoh be-cpeðen hæbbe,
⁊ ic pille þæt mine ealdoþ-menn ⁊ min þenig-menn þaþ
ealle mib synban ⁊ þis þus gebælan. þonne hæfbe ic æþ
on oðþe pisan a-pjutan ymbe ymbe (sic) myn ypfe þa ic
hæfbe maþe feoh ⁊ ma maga ⁊ hæfbe monegū mannū þa
ge-pþutu oðe-fæst ⁊ on þaþ ylcan ge-pittenesse hy pæþion
a-pþutene, þonne hæbbe ic nu foribærmeb⁵ þa ealban þe ic
ge-ahsian mihte. Gif hyria⁶ hpylc funben bið ne foþi-

---

¹ Æsctune. ² Burnan. ³ Dælde. ⁴ Frynd.
⁵ Forbærneð. ⁶ Hyra.

stent[1] þæt naht, fori[2]-þam ic pille þæt hit nu þus sy mið
godes fultume. ꒰ ic pille þa menn þe þa land habbað þa
porið ge-læstan þe on mines fæder yrfe ge-prite[3] standað,
spa spa hy fyrmest[4] magon; ꒰ ic pille gife ic ænigum menn
æniꒌ feoh unleanoð hæbbe þæt mine, magas þ hupu ꒌe-le-
anan. ꒰ ic pille þa menn þe ic mine boc-land be-cpeden
hæbbe þ hy hit ne a-syllan of minum cynne oferi heoria
dæg, ac ic pille[5] hyria dæg þæt hit gange on þa nihstan
hanð me, butan hyria hpylc bearni hæbbe, þonne is me
leofast þæt hit gange on þæt strıyneð[6] on þa præpneð
healfe þa hpile þe ænig þæs pyriðe sy. min ylbria fæðeri[7]
hæfðe ge-cpeden hys land on þa sperie-healfe nær on þa
spinl-healfe, þonne, gif ic ge-sealðe ænigrie pifhanða þ he
ge-strinðe þonne fori-gylðan mine magas, ꒰ gif hy hit he
þan libenðan habban pillan, gif hit elles sy gange hit oferi
hyria dæg spa spa þe æri ge-cpeden hæfðon, foriþon ic
cpeð' þæt hi hit gylðan, fori-þon hy foð to minum þe ic
syllan mot spa pif-hanða spa præpneð-hanða spa præpneð
hanða (sic) spað-eri ic pille. ꒰ ic bibbe on godes naman ꒰
on his halıgria þ minria[9] maga nan ne yrife-penrıða[10] ne
ge-spence nan nænıg cyriehf þaria þe ic forie-geald, ꒰ ine
pestseaxena pitan to rihte ge-riehton þæt ic hi mot lætan
spa freo spa þeope spaðeri ic pille, ac ic fori godes lufan ꒰
fori minria saple þearife pille þ hy syn heoria fricolses
pyriðe, ꒰ hyria cyries, ꒰ ic on gones hifienðes naman beoðe
þat hy nan man ne briocie ne mið feos manunge ne mið
nænꒌum þingum þ hy ne motan ceosan spylcne mann
spylce hy pillan, ꒰ ic pille þæt man agıfe þam hipum æt
ðomria-hanıne hyria lanð-bec hyria lanð-bec (sic), ꒰
hyria frieols spylce hauð to ceosenne spylce him leofast
sy, fori me, ꒰ for ælfleðe, ꒰ fori þa friynð þe heo forie
þıngoðe ꒰ ic forie þıngıe. ꒰ sec man eac on cpicum ceape
ymbe minrie saple þearife, spa hit beon mæge, ꒰ spa hit
eac ge-riysne sy ꒰ spa ge me fori-gyfan pillan.

---

[1] Forstent.   [2] Forðam.   [3] Yrfe-gewrite.   [4] Fyrmest.
[5] "Ofer" needs here to be supplied. as in Manning.
[6] Stryneð.   [7] Ylbra fæðer.   [8] Forðon ic cweðe.   [9] Minna.
[10] Yrfewearda.

" Explanatio Testamenti Alfredi Regis, de lingua Saxonica in Anglicam.

"I Alfred westsaxene kyng wyth goddys ȝyft, and by thy wyttenesse I seye nowe the intention of my last wylle to be fulfyllyd aftyr my day.   Fyrst I grawnte to Edward my yldiste sone the londes at stratnet in triconschyre and hortyngtune and all the frelond that leof hath hold, and that lond at carumtune and at kylfantune, and at burnham and at wedmore, and I conferme to the keper[1] at Ceodre tha he hyt have aftyr the puyngtyng that we erst seyde hafe w[t] that land at kyntune and that ther to longyth, and I to hym grawnte the londis at kantintune and at bedewynde and at pefesy and at hysseburn and at suttune and at leodridan and at aultune and alle the frelond that I iu kent have, and at nether hysseburn and at kyseldene. I ȝyve my chef servant at wynchester after the syne-ment that hyt my fadyr er beqweythyd and myn other fee that I to egulfe gafe un to at certeyn tyme at the nether hysseborne.   And that my ȝongyr sone have that lond at Ederingtune and that at the dene, and that at Mene and at Ambresbury and at deone and at sturemynster and at ȝeule and at kruerne and at whytchyrche and at axamuntham and at brauescumbe and at kolumtune and at twyfyrd and at Myllenburn, and at Exanmynster and at sutheswyrthe and at lyntune and the lond that there to longyth the whyche be all that I undyr hevyn have uttake Trikonschyre.   ¶And to my ilderyst dowthter I grawnt the twune of welewe, and to the mydmest dowther I

---

[1] Mr. Manning translates this clause thus:—"And I am a petitioner to the families at Ceodre that they him would chuse on the condition that we formerly expressed had," &c.; and he adds this note: "These hipar 'families,' at Chedder, were the ceorls who occupied the tenemental lands there.   They were so far analogous to those who, in the succeed-ing feudal times, were called 'privileged villains,' as that they could not be compelled to hold their lands against their own consent.   Hence it was that Alfred had stipulated with them, on the ground of a requisition on his part, to chuse Edward his Son to be their landlord; i. e., to con-tinue his tenants after he himself should be dead and gone."

graunte the twunc of klerc and of kendevere, and to my
ʒongyst dowthtyr I graunte the twune of welyg and of
Aʌcktunc and of schyppcuam. ¶And to Athelmc my
brotherys sonc I grawnt the twunc of Eleyngburn and
of kumptunc and of krundelc and of bedyngum and of
bedyngham and of burnham and of thunresfeld an of
Aschengum. ¶And to athelwold my brotherys sone the
twunc of godelmyngc and of gylford and of stemugum.
¶And to osferthc my cosyn I graunte the twuue of bec-
canle and of Rytherhamfeld and of dyccanlyngum and of
suttunc and of lullyngarynster and of Angemeryngum and
of Felthham and the lond that there to longyth. ¶And
to Alswythe the twnc of lamburne and of wantyngh and
of Ethandunc. ¶And to my twey sonys I beqweyth a
thwsund pund Eythyr fyf hundryd pund. ¶And to myn
ilderyst dowʒter and to the myddelyst and to the ʒongyst
and to Alswythe to hem fowr fowrhundyrd pund everyche
of hem an hunderyd pund. ¶And to everych of my
gentylmen an hunderyd mark. ¶And to Ethelmc and
Athelwoldc and Osferthc also everyche of hem an hunderyd
mark. ¶And to Ethered my gentylman I ʒyve a swerd
and twenti hunderyd mark. ¶And to that man that
folwyth me wyt wham at Estyrtyd I covenaunt made
I take too hunderyd pund that man to ʒyve and that man
to partye be twyxt all tho ther hym to be byryyd
lykyth after the wyse that I now to hym dele. ¶And to
the Erchebyschop I ʒyve an hunderyd mark and Esne
byschop and werferthc byschop and to hym of schyrburn
everyche of hem as myche for to departye and to dele for
me and for my fadyr and for that thyng that he (*sic* for ' I ')
before asynyd. And I asyne too hunderyd pund to fyfty
masse prestys twrw all my Recm. And fifti schilyngys
to every of godys servauntys, and fyfty schylyng to dele
amonge the powr peple and fyfty to the chyrche wher
that I am byryyd. ¶And I not nat trewely weyther ther
ys more than these ʒyftys ne I trow that there ys no
more as I wene. Yf yt more be, be hyt all demenyd as I
to ʒyve have seyd. ¶And I wyll that my gentylmen and
my ʒymen and al tho that wyth hem beth that they thys

thus departye ne on none other wyse than I have wryte
by fore to fore my heyr to wham I have most ȝyve and
most myȝt. And monymen han at thys tyme ther to
wryte and to fore all thys wyttenesse thes yyftes were
i wryte than have I now for chargyd the pryncys of my
Reeme that I aske myȝt of hem that fundyn byth that
hyt let not for that that hyt ys my wyll that hyt nw be
thus thorw goddys strenkth. And I wyl that tho men
the whyche these londys havyn kepe the word that of
my faderys herytage stondyth i wryte of myche as they
strengyst mowe. And I wyll yf I eny man have gyfe or
eny lenyd have that they to my cosynis or to here hyt
seue. And I wyll that tho men that I my freland have
beqwethyd that they ȝyve hyt nat from my kynne overe
here day. And I wyll And I wyll (sic) that aftyr here
day to the next hond of me, wythowte hem that chyldryn
have, than ys me levyst that hyt go to the mawl chyld
hy gete as long whyle as eny on erthe be. Myn yldyr
fadyr hys lond on the same wyse be qweythyd to the
mawlys. An than yf I take hyt on eny degre to wom-
mennys hond I wyll that aftyr here day he to ȝelde hyt
to my mawlys kyn the whyche comyn of here. And yf
they by here lyf lyvynge hyt will have ; and yf hyt ell
be, than go hyt ovyr here day so as we here byfore have
be qweythyd. Ferthermore I sey that they hyt ȝelde for
the lyvelode of my kyn to whem I ȝeve most whether
they ben mayde chyldryn or sonys as me best lykyth
and I bydde on goddys name and on all halewene that
none of my kyn here aftyrward labor not aȝenst eny of
ther kynrede that I have ȝyve and be qweythyd to, here
byfore. And w^t me all the worthynesse of west saxone
to ryȝt consentyn that I most leve hem as fre as thowt
wheythyr that I wyll, and I for goddys love and for my
sowle helthe wylle that they in possessyon of here fredom
and alle here kyred, and I on goddys holy name comawnde
that them no man wythsey nother w^t strenthe nother
w^t eny thyng that they ne mote sesyn what man wham
they wylle in here londys. ¶And I wyll than (sic) men
ȝeve to the hows at domrahamme here land bok and here

fredomys hem to scosyn what hond hem levyst is, for me
and for Elflede and for here frendys that he ys bownd to
and that I am bounde to and for the nedy that alyve be
to kepe hyt that yt may be helthe for my sowle, and
that hyt be to me in forȝyvenesse and so I desyre me to
be for ȝeve."

BIBLIOGRAPHICAL PUBLICATIONS

OF

MESSRS. TRÜBNER & CO.

60, PATERNOSTER ROW, LONDON.

IMPORTANT TO

Librarians, Collectors of Books, & Booksellers.

In Two Volumes, 8vo., pp. 1950 of Letter-press, Seven Chromo-Lithographic Plates of Binding-Specimens, Sixteen fac-simile Plates of Papyri and Early Types, numerous Woodcuts, etc. Price £2 : 8s.; Large Paper, £4 : 4s.

MEMOIRS OF LIBRARIES:

INCLUDING

A Practical Handbook of Library Economy.

By EDWARD EDWARDS.

Table of Contents.

PART I.—HISTORY OF LIBRARIES.

(IN FIVE BOOKS.)

OPINIONS OF THE PRESS.

" Of the industry bestowed upon this extensive compilation, and of the marvellous condensation of fact which it supplies, it is difficult to speak in terms of proper commendation; even to the most accomplished bibliographer it cannot fail to be of great service, but how much more to the tyro or ordinary bibliographer."—*Brownson's Review.*

" There is more variety, interest, and even life, in the Memoirs of Libraries, than might be expected. Mr. Edwards has a more comprehensive mind and a more sensible judgment than always characterise the tribe of librarii. His style has not an undue spirit of rhetoric, which throws off anything approaching to the manner of Dryasdust."—*Spectator.*

" Both as a history of libraries and a manual of their economy, this work is valuable: delightful to the scholar in the first respect; in the second, indispensable to the librarian."—*Critic.*

" We now take leave of these volumes, feeling that we have given a very imperfect indication of their contents, and strongly recommend them to the consideration of all persons connected with or interested in libraries, public or private, because they contain a vast quantity of information never before collected, and much that would be sought for in vain elsewhere."—*Bookseller.*

" Mr. Edwards's style is pleasant, and free from the slang and pedantry of many more costly productions in the field of bibliography. If we feel occasionally inclined to differ from the author's views and deductions, we do so at all times with some deference, because throughout the work it is evident that he has been earnest to furnish the fullest and most satisfactory information which it was in his power to do."—*Leader.*

" It is now generally conceded that the civilization of a people may be judged rather by the number and value of its private libraries, than by the extent and magnificence of those provided by the Sovereign. Such being the case, it is incumbent upon us to examine our position in this particular, by comparison with other nations, This we are now enabled to do, for the first time, by the aid afforded in Mr. Edwards's ' Memoirs of Libraries,' which exhibits a mass of evidence such as only the greatest devotion to the subject, perseveringly continued through many years, could have accumulated. So completely is the subject exhausted, that it would be vain and useless for the inquirer to push his researches further in order to obtain a clear view of the libraries of the past and present; for what of interest or value he finds not in these volumes he will scarcely hope to obtain elsewhere."—*Gentleman's Magazine.*

" The various schemes propounded for the classification of knowledge—the extent to which libraries may safely be made available for public use—their internal economy, and the qualifications essential for their management—these are subjects which it would have afforded us both pleasure and profit to have discussed with Mr. Edwards. But it is time to take leave of him with the respect due to a writer whom some diffuseness, occasional want of discrimination, and a few doubtful views, will not debar from a cordial reception wherever industry is appreciated or erudition recognised."—*Press.*

IMPORTANT WORK ON ENGLISH AND AMERICAN LITERARY HISTORY.

𝔄 𝔆𝔯𝔦𝔱𝔦𝔠𝔞𝔩 𝔇𝔦𝔠𝔱𝔦𝔬𝔫𝔞𝔯𝔶 𝔬𝔣 𝔈𝔫𝔤𝔩𝔦𝔰𝔥 𝔏𝔦𝔱𝔢𝔯𝔞𝔱𝔲𝔯𝔢,

AND BRITISH AND AMERICAN AUTHORS,

LIVING AND DECEASED, FROM THE EARLIEST ACCOUNTS TO THE MIDDLE OF THE NINETEENTH CENTURY.

Containing 31,000 *Biographies and Literary Notices.   With an Index of Subject Matter.*

By S. AUSTIN ALLIBONE.

The Second Volume (letter K. to Z, likewise exceeding 1000 pp.), which is in a very forward state (being stereotyped as far as the letter S), will complete the work, and be published, with a most elaborate Index of Subject-Matter, in the Autumn of 1859, on the same terms as the first Volume.

The above important work was originally announced to be published in 1857, in one Volume, imperial 8vo., of about 1500 pages, and the first appeal to the public on its behalf was signally successful. The delay in the publication seems to have caused a feeling of disappointment among the patrons of the work, but it is hoped that this feeling will give way to one of lively satisfaction when the first half of it is examined. The high expectations raised by the mere announcement made it incumbent upon the Author and Publishers to spare no expense or trouble to bring the work to the greatest state of perfection; and although stereotyped to the letter II at the time it was first announced, that portion has been entirely revised, partly rewritten, and so much new matter introduced, that the subscribers will now receive above 2000 pages, at no increase of price.

DESCRIPTIVE TITLE.

THE characteristics of the work, which have not been united in any previous undertaking of the kind, are as follow :—

" 1. It is a Biographical Dictionary of English and American Authors, comprising both the living and the dead; furnishing those incidents respecting the persons who have made themselves famous in the Republic of Letters, which every reader desires to know, and few know where to find.

" 2. It is a Bibliographical Manual, giving information as to the best editions of authors, the circumstances attending their publication, the reception which they met with from the public, the influence they have exercised on the public mind, and many other interesting particulars, not one of which the true lover of books and student of letters would 'willingly let die.'

" As a Bibliographical Manual, the Index, which forms the second portion of the volume, will prove no small addition to its value. In this Index the subjects of human knowledge are divided into forty distinct classes, and an alphabet is allotted to each. By this means the reader is enabled to see at a glance who are the principal writers on all subjects, from Agriculture, Class 1st, to Voyages, Class 40th.

TRÜBNER'S BIBLIOGRAPHICAL GUIDE—*continued.*

This work, it is believed is the first attempt to marshal the Literature of the United States of America during the last forty years, according to the generally received bibliographical canons. The Librarian will welcome it, no doubt, as a companion volume to Brunet, Lowndes and Ebert, whilst to the bookseller it will be a faithful guide to the American branch of English Literature—a branch which, on account of its rapid increase and rising importance, begins to force itself daily more and more upon his attention. Nor will the work be of less interest to the man of letters, inasmuch as it comprises complete Tables of Contents to all the more prominent Collections of the Americans, to the Journals, Memoirs, Proceedings and Transactions of their learned Societies—and thus furnishes an intelligible key to a department of American scientific activity hitherto but imperfectly known and understood in Europe.

A HANDBOOK OF AFRICAN, AUSTRALIAN, AND POLYNESIAN PHILOLOGY,

As represented in the Library of His Excellency Sir George Grey, K.C.B.

HER MAJESTY'S HIGH COMMISSIONER OF THE CAPE COLONY.

CLASSED, ANNOTATED, AND EDITED BY

SIR GEORGE GREY AND DR. W. H. J. BLEEK.

Vol. I. Part 1.—South Africa, 8vo. pp. 186. 7s. 6d.

Vol. I. Part 2.—Africa (North of the Tropic of Capricorn), 8vo. pp. 70. 2s.

Vol. II. Part 1.—Australia, 8vo. pp. iv., 44. 1s. 6d.

Vol. II. Part 2.—Papuan Languages of the Loyalty Islands and New Hebrides, comprising those of the Islands of Nengone, Lifu, Anciteum, Tana, and others, 8vo. pp. 12. 6d.

Vol. II. Part 3.—Fiji Islands and Rotuma (with Supplement to Part 2, Papuan Languages, and Part 1, Australia.) 8vo. pp. 34. 1s.

Vol. II. Part 4.—New Zealand, the Chatham Islands, and Auckland Islands, 8vo. pp. 76. 3s. 6d.

Vol. II. Part 4 (*Continuation*).—Polynesia and Borneo, 8vo. pp. 77 to 154. 3s. 6d.

The above is, without exception, the most important addition yet made to African Philology. The amount of materials brought together by Sir George, with a view to elucidate the subject, is stupendous; and the labour bestowed on them, and the results arrived at, incontestably establish the claim of the Author to be called the father of African and Polynesian Philology.

OPINIONS OF THE PRESS.

"We congratulate the Governor of the Cape on the production of a most important aid to the study of the twin sciences of philology and ethnology, and look forward to the completion of the Catalogue itself as a great and permanent step towards civilization of the barbarous races whose formation, habits, language, religion, and food, are all, more or less, most carefully noted in its pages."— *Leader.*

"It is for these substantial reasons that we deemed it worth a brief notice to call attention to these excellently arranged Catalogues (with important notes), describing the various works in the library of Sir George Grey, and by which this great philanthropist will greatly aid in civilizing the numerous peoples within the limit of the colony of the Cape of Good Hope."—*Brighton Gazette.*

TRÜBNER'S BIBLIOTHECA GLOTTICA.

THE LITERATURE

OF

AMERICAN ABORIGINAL LANGUAGES.

By HERMANN E. LUDEWIG.

With Additions and Corrections by Professor WM. W. TURNER.

Edited by NICOLAS TRÜBNER.

8vo.; fly and general Title, 2 leaves; Dr. Ludewig's Preface, pp. v—viii; Editors' Preface, pp. ix—xii; Biographical Memoir of Dr. Ludewig, pp. xiii, xiv; and Introductory Bibliographical Notices, pp. xiv—xxiv, followed by List of Contents. Then follow Dr. Ludewig's Bibliotheca Glottica, alphabetically arranged, with additions by the Editor, pp. 1—209; Professor Turner's additions, with those of the Editor to the same, also alphabetically arranged, pp. 210—246; Index. pp. 247—256; and list of Errata, pp. 257, 258. One volume, handsomely bound in cloth, price 10s. 6d.

This work is intended to supply a great want, now that the study of Ethnology has proved that exotic languages are not mere curiosities, but essential and interesting parts of the natural history of man, forming one of the most curious links in the great chain of national affinities, defining as they do the reciprocity existing between man and the soil he lives upon. No one can venture to write the history of America without a knowledge of her aboriginal languages; and unimportant as such researches may seem to men engaged in the mere bustling occupations of life, they will at least acknowledge that these records of the past, like the stern-lights of a departing ship, are the last glimmers of savage life, as it becomes absorbed or recedes before the tide of civilization. Dr. Ludewig and Professor Turner have made most diligent use of the public and private collections in America, access to all of which was most liberally granted to them. This has placed at their disposal the labours of the American Missionaries, so little known on this side of the Atlantic that they may be looked upon almost in the light of untrodden ground. But English and Continental libraries have also been ransacked; and Dr. Ludewig kept up a constant and active correspondence with scholars of "the Fatherland," as well as with men of similar tastes and pursuits in France, Spain, and Holland, determined to leave no stone unturned to render his labours as complete as possible. The volume, perfect in itself, is the first of an enlarged edition of Vater's "*Linguarum totius orbis Index.*" The work has been noticed by the press of both Continents, and we may be permitted to refer particularly to the following:

OPINIONS OF THE PRESS.

" This work, mainly the production of the late Herr Ludewig, a German naturalized in America, is devoted to an account of the literature of the aboriginal languages of that country. It gives an alphabetical list of the various tribes of whose languages any record remains, and refers to the works, papers, or manuscripts, in which such information may be found. The work has evidently been a labour of love; and as no pains seems to have been spared by the editors, Prof. Turner and Mr. Trübner, in rendering the work as

TRÜBNER'S BIBLIOTHECA GLOTTICA—*continued.*

accurate and complete as possible, those who are most interested in its contents will be best able to judge of the labour and assiduity bestowed upon it by author, editors, and publisher."—*Athenæum*, 5th April, 1858.

"This is the first instalment of a work which will be of the greatest value to philologists ; and is a compendium of the aboriginal languages of the American continents, and a digest of all the known literature bearing upon those languages. Mr. Trübner's hand has been engaged *passim*, and in his preface he lays claim to about one-sixth of the whole ; and we have no doubt that the encouragement with which this portion of the work will be received by scholars, will be such as to inspire Mr. Trübner with sufficient confidence to persevere in his arduous and most honourable task "—*The Critic*, 15th Dec. 1857.

"Few would believe that a good octavo volume would be necessary to exhaust the subject; yet so it is, and this handsome, useful, and curious volume, carefully compiled by Mr. Ludewig, assisted by Professor Turner, and edited by the careful hand of Mr. Trübner, the well-known publisher, will be sure to find a place in many libraries."—*Bent's Advertiser*, 6th Nov. 1857.

"The lovers of American linguistics will find in the work of Mr. Trübner scarcely any point omitted calculated to aid the comparative philologer in tracing the various languages of the great Western Continent."—*Galway Mercury*, 30th Jan. 1858.

"Only those deeply versed in philological studies can appreciate this book at its full value. It shows that there are upwards of seven hundred and fifty aboriginal American languages." — *Gentleman's Magazine*, Feb. 1858.

"The work contains an account of no fewer than seven hundred different aboriginal dialects of America, with an introductory chapter of bibliographical information ; and under each dialect is an account of any grammars or other works illustrative of it."—*The Bookseller,* Jan. 1858.

"We have here the list of monuments still existing of an almost innumerable series of languages and dialects of the American Continent. The greater part of Indian grammars and vocabularies exist only in MS., and were compiled chiefly by Missionaries of the Christian Church; and to Dr. Ludewig and Mr. Trübner, we are, therefore, the more indebted for the great care with which they have pointed out where such are to be found, as well as for enumerating those which have been printed, either in a separate shape, in

collections, or in voyages and travels, and elsewhere."—*Leader*, 11th Sept. 1858.

"I have not time, nor is it my purpose, to go into a review of this admirable work, or to attempt to indicate the extent and value of its contents. It is, perhaps, enough to say, that apart from a concise but clear enumeration and notice of the various general philological works which treat with greater or less fulness of American languages, or which incidentally touch upon their bibliography, it contains not less than 256 closely-printed octavo pages of bibliographical notices of grammars, vocabularies, etc., of the aboriginal languages of America. It is a peculiar and valuable feature of the work that not only the titles of printed or published grammars or vocabularies are given, but also that unpublished or MS. works of these kinds are noticed in all cases where they are known to exist, but which have disappeared among the *débris* of the suppressed convents and religious establishments of Spanish America." —*E.' G. Squier, in a paper read before the American Ethnological Society,* 12th Jan. 1858.

"In consequence of the death of the author before he had finished the revisal of the work, it has been carefully examined by competent scholars, who have also made many valuable additions."—*American Publishers' Circular*, 30th Jan. 1858.

"It contains 256 closely-printed pages of titles of printed books and manuscripts, and notices of American aboriginal languages, and embraces references to nearly all that has been written or published respecting them, whether in special works or incidentally in books of travel, periodicals, or proceedings of learned societies."—*New York Herald*, 29th Jan. 1858.

"The manner in which this contribution to the bibliography of American languages has been executed, both by the author, Mr. Ludewig, and the able writers who have edited the work since his death, is spoken of in the highest terms by gentlemen most conversant with the subject."—*American Historical Magazine*, Vol. II., No. 5, May, 1858.

"Je terminerai en annonçant le premier volume d'une publication appelée à rendre de grands services à la philologie comparée et à la linguistique générale. Je veux parler de la Bibliotheca Glottica, ouvrage devant renfermer la liste de tous les dictionnaires et de toutes les grammaires des langues connues, tant imprimés que manuscrits. L'éditeur, de cette précieuse bibliographie est M. Nicolas Trübner, dont le nom est honorablement connu dans le monde oriental. Le

TRÜBNER'S BIBLIOTHECA GLOTTICA—*continued.*

premier volume est consacré aux idiomes Américaines; le second doit traiter des langues de l'Inde. Le travail est fait avec le soin le plus consciencieux, et fera honneur à M. Nicolas Trübner, surtout s'il poursuit son œuvre avec le même ardeur qu'il mise à le commencer."—*L. Léon de Rosny, Revue de l'Orient, Février,* 1858.

" Mr. Trübner's most important work on the bibliography of the aboriginal languages of America is deserving of all praise, as eminently useful to those who study that branch of literature. The value, too, of the book, and of the pains which its compilation must have cost, will not be lessened by the consideration that it is first in this field of linguistic literature." — *Petermann's Geographische Mittheilungen*, p. 79, Feb. 1858.

" Undoubtedly this volume of Trübner's Bibliotheca Glottica ranks amongst the most valuable additions which of late years have enriched our bibliographical literature. To us Germans it is most gratifying that the initiative has been taken by a German bookseller himself, one of the most intelligent and active of our countrymen abroad, to produce a work which has higher aims than mere pecuniary profit, and that he, too, has laboured at its production with his own hands; because daily it is becoming a circumstance of rarer occurrence that, as in this case, it is a bookseller's primary object to serve the cause of literature rather than to enrich himself." — *P. Trömel, Börsenblatt*, 4th Jan. 1858.

. " In the compilation of the work the editors have availed themselves not only of the labours of Vater, Barton, Duponceau, Gallatin, De Souza, and others, but also of the MS. sources left by the missionaries, and of many books of which even the library of the British Museum is deficient, and furnish the fullest account of the literature of no less than 525 languages. The value of the work, so necessary to the study of ethnology, is greatly enhanced by the addition of a good Index." —*Berliner National-Zeitung*, 22nd Nov. 1857.

" The name of the author, to all those who are acquainted with his former works, and who know the thoroughness and profound character of his investigations, is a sufficient guarantee that this work will be one of standard authority, and one that will fully answer the demands of the present time."— *Petzholdt's Anzeiger*, Jan. 1858.

" The chief merit of the editor and publisher is to have terminated the work carefully and lucidly in contents and form, and thus to have established a new and 'largely augmented edition of " *Vater's Linguarum totius orbis Index*," after Professor Jülg's revision of 1847. In order to continue and complete this work the editor requires the assistance of all those who are acquainted with this new branch of science, and we sincerely hope it may be accorded to him."— *Magazin für die Literatur des Auslandes*, No. 38, 1858.

" As the general title of the book indicates, it will be extended to the languages of the other Continents in case it meet with a favourable reception, which we most cordially wish it."—*A. F. Pott., Preussische Jahrbücher*, Vol. II. part 1.

" Cette compilation savante est sans contredit, le travail bibliographique le plus important que notre époque ait vu surgir sur les nations indigènes de l'Amérique." — *Nouvelles Annales des Voyages.* Avril, 1859.

" La Bibliotheca Glottica, dont M. Nicolas Trübner a commencé la publication, est un des livres les plus utiles qui aient jamais été rédigés pour faciliter l'étude de la philologie comparée. Le premier tome de cette grande bibliographie linguistique comprend la liste textuelle de toutes les grammaires, de tous les dictionnaires et des vocabulaires même les moins étendus qui ont été imprimés dans les différents dialectes des deux Amériques; en outre, il fait connaître les ouvrages manuscrits de la même nature renfermés dans les principales bibliothèques publiques et particulières. Ce travail a dû nécessiter de longues et patientes recherches; aussi mérite-t-il d'attirer tout particulièrement l'attention des philologues. Puissent les autres volumes de cette bibliothèque être rédigés avec le même soin et se trouver bientôt entre les mains de tous les savants auxquels ils peuvent rendre des services inappréciables."— *Revue Américaine et Orientale*, No. I., Oct. 1858.

The Editor has also received most kind and encouraging letters respecting the work from Sir George Grey, the Chevalier Bunsen, Dr. Th. Goldstucker, Mr. Watts (of the Museum), Professor A. Fr. Pott (of Halle), Dr. Julius Petzholt (of Dresden), Hofrath Dr. Grasse (of Dresden), M. F. F. de la Figaniere (of Lisbon), E. Edwards (of Manchester), Dr. Max Müller (of Oxford), Dr. Buschmann (of Berlin), Dr. Jülg (of Cracow), and other linguistic scholars.

TRÜBNER'S BIBLIOTHECA TECHNICA: A SUBJECT-MATTER INDEX TO THE PUBLISHED INVENTIONS OF ALL NATIONS, 1823 TO 1853 INCLUSIVE. In 1 vol. 8vo., pp. viii., 26, xvi. 1050. 24s.

The object of this work is to record in the form of a Dictionary the Literature of Technology and its kindred branches, dispersed over the different Journals and Magazines of all Nations.

In the Press,

MAPOTECA COLOMBIANA: CATALOGO DE TODOS LOS MAPAS, PLANOS, VISTAS, ETC., RELATIVOS A LA AMERICA-ESPAÑOLA, BRASIL, E ISLAS ADYACENTES. Por el Dr. Ezequiel Uricoechea, de Bogota, Nueva Granada. 1 vol. 8vo.

A very useful companion to all works relating to the Bibliography of America.

BIBLIOTHEQUE AMERICAINE: OU CATALOGUE RAISONNÉ D'UNE PRECIEUSE COLLECTION DE LIVRES RELATIFS A L'AMERIQUE QUI ONT PARU DEPUIS SA DECOUVERTE JUSQU'A L'AN 1700. Par Paul Troemel. 8vo.

Amongst the 556 articles of which the Collection consists, at least 100 are not mentioned by any bibliographer. Indeed, only about 150 of them are found in Ternaux and Rich, which of itself is ample testimony of the importance, and must secure to the publication more than ordinary interest in the eyes of bibliographers and literary men.

TRÜBNER'S BIBLIOTHECA JAPONICA: A DESCRIPTIVE LIST OF BOOKS ILLUSTRATIVE OF JAPAN AND THE JAPANESE, FROM 1542 TO THE PRESENT TIME. Edited, with Critical and Historical Notes, by Dr. G. M. Asher.

The above work cannot fail to prove of great interest now that Japan is thrown open for European enterprise. The best Dutch, German, Portuguese, Spanish, Italian, French, English, Russian, and American Authorities, have been consulted in its production.

TRÜBNER & CO.,
60, PATERNOSTER ROW, LONDON.